Annual Conference of the Nations of the Americas Chapter of the Association for Computational Linguistics (NAACL 2025)

Tutorial Abstracts

Albuquerque, New Mexico, USA
1 May 2025

ISBN: 979-8-3313-1908-3

Printed from e-media with permission by:

Curran Associates, Inc.
57 Morehouse Lane
Red Hook, NY 12571

Some format issues inherent in the e-media version may also appear in this print version.

Printed with permission by Curran Associates, Inc. (2026)

For permission requests, please contact the Association for Computational Linguistics at the address below.

Association for Computational Linguistics
209 N. Eighth Street
Stroudsburg, Pennsylvania 18360

Phone: 1-570-476-8006
Fax: 1-570-476-0860

acl@aclweb.org

Additional copies of this publication are available from:

Curran Associates, Inc.
57 Morehouse Lane
Red Hook, NY 12571 USA
Phone: 845-758-0400
Fax: 845-758-2633
Email: curran@proceedings.com
Web: www.proceedings.com

NAACL 2025

The 2025 Annual Conference of the Nations of the Americas Chapter of the Association for Computational Linguistics: Human Language Technologies

Tutorial Abstracts

May 1, 2025

Order copies of this and other ACL proceedings from:

Association for Computational Linguistics (ACL)
317 Sidney Baker St. S
Suite 400 - 134
Kerrville, TX 78028
USA
Tel: +1-855-225-1962
acl@aclweb.org

Introduction

Welcome to the tutorial session of NAACL 2025!

We are thrilled to welcome you to this year's NAACL tutorial session, a cornerstone event of the conference. Our tutorials offer a deep dive into a diverse range of cutting-edge and emerging topics, presented by leading researchers at the forefront of their fields. These sessions are designed to equip you with the latest insights, tools, and methodologies, enriching your understanding of the ever-evolving landscape of computational linguistics and natural language processing.

Continuing our longstanding tradition, the call, submission, review, and selection processes for tutorials were jointly coordinated across NAACL, ACL, and EMNLP. The review committee comprised the NAACL tutorial chairs (Rui Zhang, Swabha Swayamdipta, and Maria Lomeli), the ACL tutorial chairs (Yuki Arase, David Jurgens, and Fei Xia), and the interim EMNLP tutorial chairs (Jessy Li and Fei Liu). Each tutorial proposal underwent a thorough evaluation by a panel of two to three reviewers, who assessed the submissions based on several key criteria: clarity and preparedness, novelty and timeliness of the topic, instructors' experience, anticipated audience interest, commitment to open access teaching materials, and diversity considerations—including multilingualism, gender, age, and geographic representation—as well as compatibility with the preferred conference venue.

This year, we received a remarkable total of 76 tutorial submissions, from which 8 were selected for presentation at NAACL. These tutorials promise to offer engaging and informative sessions, catering to a broad spectrum of interests and expertise levels within the computational linguistics and NLP community.

We deeply appreciate the contributions of all tutorial authors, as well as the tireless efforts and strong collaboration of the conference organizers—with special thanks to General Chair Colin Cherry for his exceptional leadership.

We hope these tutorials provide valuable insights and contribute meaningfully to your overall experience at the conference. Wishing you an inspiring and engaging time at NAACL 2025, filled with learning and connection!

Warm regards,
NAACL 2025 Tutorial Co-Chairs,
Swabha Swayamdipta
Maria Lomeli
Rui Zhang

Organizing Committee

General Chair

Colin Cherry, Google

Program Chairs

Luis Chiruzzo, Universidad de la República
Alan Ritter, Georgia Institute of Technology
Lu Wang, University of Michigan

Tutorial Chairs

Rui Zhang, Penn State University
Swabha Swayamdipta, University of Southern California
Maria Lomeli, Meta

Table of Contents

Creative Planning with Language Models: Practice, Evaluation and Applications

Alexander Spangher[1] **Tenghao Huang**[1] **Philippe Laban**[2] **Nanyun Peng**[3]
[1]University of Southern California
[2]Microsoft Research
[3] University of California, Los Angeles
spangher@usc.edu, tenghaoh@usc.edu, philippe.laban@microsoft.com, vnpeng@ucla.edu

Abstract

The use of large language models (LLMs) in human-centered creative domains — such as journalism, scientific writing, and storytelling — has showcased their potential for content generation but highlighted a critical gap: planning. Planning, a fundamental process in many creative domains, refers to higher level decisions writers (or agents) make that influence textual output they produce. Planning is especially hard to perform in creative domains, where human rewards are often unclear or sparsely observed. This tutorial explores how planning has been learned and deployed in creative workflows. We will cover three aspects of creativity: **Problem-Finding** (how to define rewards and goals for creative tasks), **Path-Finding** (how to generate novel creative outputs that meet goals) and **Evaluation** (how to judge). We will also consider three learning settings: *Full Data Regimens* (when observational data for decisions and resulting text exist), *Partial* (when text exists but decisions can be inferred) and *Low* (when neither exist). The tutorial will end with practical demonstrations in computational journalism, web agents, and other creative domains. By bridging theoretical concepts and practical demonstrations, this tutorial aims to inspire new research directions in leveraging LLMs for creative planning tasks.

1 Introduction

LLMs have demonstrated impressive generative capacities across a range of tasks. However, many human creative tasks (e.g. in journalism, scientific writing, video script writing and creative story generation) involve extensive planning. For example, a human journalist typically follows a multi-step process before they are even *ready* to write a news article (e.g. *"find story idea"* → *"develop angle"* → *"find informational sources"* → *"get quotes"* → *"confirm facts"*) (Cohen et al., 2011). An emerging body of work has pointed to key short-comings of LLMs and opportunities for progress in domains where planning is required, actions need to be taken and objectives are poorly defined.

Many emerging tasks in NLP can be framed as "planning" tasks: either those that are explicitly using LLMs as planning-agents (e.g. (Zhou et al., 2023)) or those that attempt to infer or learn from the plans guiding human text generation (Spangher et al., 2024a). In this tutorial, we aim to bring tasks in this umbrella into dialogue. Can the ability to plan make LLMs become more useful, more human-like and more attuned to the needs of diverse creative professionals? We aim to consolidate an emerging direction of work that lies in the intersection of: creative generation, agentic planning, and human-centered NLP.

2 Three Aspects of Creativity

The main structure of our tutorial breaks down creative planning into three main stages: Problem-Finding, Path-Finding and Evaluation. Each section is grounded in a large history cognitive science literature. We cover each stage in turn.

2.1 Problem-Finding

> "The formulation of a problem is often more essential than its solution, which may be merely a matter of mathematical or experimental skill."
>
> *Einstein and Infeld (1938), The Evolution of Physics*

In their seminal work, Getzels and Csikszentmihalyi (1976) studied art students, and observed that those who focused most on *defining the problem* produced more creative work. The *problem-finding* domain of creativity research has since expanded to include various ways that creative actors define tasks, goal-states and rewards.

We map *problem-finding* broadly, in NLP, to Learning *complex rewards*. A key question is: how can we build systems that define their own reward

Proceedings of the 2025 Annual Conference of the Nations of the Americas Chapter of the Association for Computational Linguistics: Human Language Technologies: Tutorial Abstracts, pages 1–9

functions, understand fuzzily observed rewards or mix multiple rewards for one cohesive output? We will frame several advances in language modeling in this lens. We will look at approaches that mix multiple rewards (Shi et al., 2024), framing of language modeling as inverse-reinforcement learning (IRL) (Wulfmeier et al., 2024), and explicit *emulation learning* settings.

What is emulation learning? In cognitive science, key work has been done to observe how humans (and chimpanzees) learn rewards (Hopper, 2010). In such *emulation learning* settings, humans attempt to observe and understand the *motivations and rewards* of other humans relying not just on observing the actions of others, but also upon observing the *end-state outputs* of human processes. For example, when we, as scientists, read research papers, we are often able to "read through the lines" to guess actions that were taken, even if they are not explicitly mentioned – e.g. implementation decisions, negative results, or hyperparameter sweeps (without this ability, reproducibility in our field would be nearly impossible). Another domain is shown in Figure 1, where the decision-making other humans employ prior to writing a news article can often be inferred through discourse markers (Spangher et al., a). Computer science work focused on *emulation learning* typically seeks to explicitly uncover human actions from observed text (e.g. in news articles (Spangher et al., 2024b) and in scientific writing (Starace et al., 2025)). The key in these approaches is, after uncovering these actions, is to then use them to learn rewards from human behavior at scale, utilizing frameworks like IRL (Abbeel and Ng, 2004). In this talk, we will explore how these approaches can uncover human values, motivations and rewards.

2.2 Path-Finding

> "Creativity involves breaking out of established patterns to look at things in a different way."
>
> *de Bono (1992), Serious Creativity*

Defining creativity as *how humans develop alternative methods for solving problems* have been a dominant thread in creativity research (Runco, 2001), dating to the 1950s, when J.P. Guilford addressed the American Psychological Association (Guilford, 1950). Guilford and other psychologists developed theories of creativity centered on *path-finding*, where humans engage in alternative uses (Guilford et al., 1978), exploration (Finke,

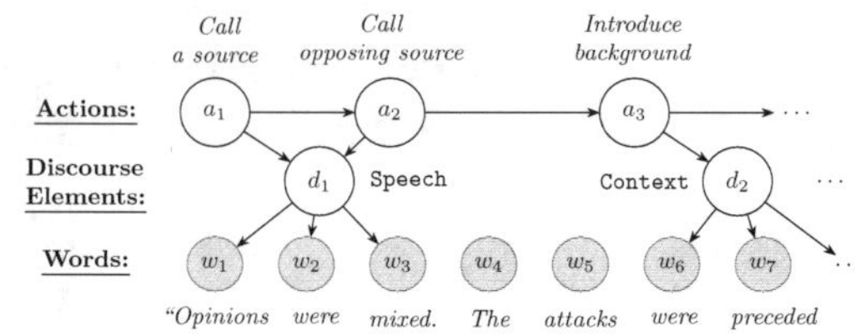

Figure 1: An example of a creative-planning task, in computational journalism: specifically, planning which sources and other forms of background information to use. Actions taken by humans while they write (i.e. a_1, a_2..) are implied through discourse acts (d_1, d_2...), which are inferred from the written text (w_1, w_2,...). This insight, and it's application across domains, allows us to infer higher-level human rewards and train agents to understand human creative processes.

1996) and metaphor (Gentner and Wolff, 2014) to come up with more inventive solutions to problems. We will explore ways computer scientists have extended such directions.

Forwards approaches Forward approaches to planning assume that we can directly train or prompt a model to generate sequences of actions. Researchers typically take an approach that involves prompt-engineering and in-context learning (Tian et al., 2024b). We will discuss some of the drawbacks of these approaches, including biases that might be introduced and reasoning failures in modeling. On the other hand, researchers with access to more data usually include enough training data to explicitly train planning agents. This can include directly planning a chain-of-thought reasoner (Chen et al., 2024b) or a environment with clearly defined reward (e.g. a tool-usage platform) (Côté et al., 2018; Shridhar et al., 2020, 2021; Huang et al., 2023; Tian et al., 2024b; Song et al., 2024). These approaches typically fall into an area of reinforcement learning referred to as imitation learning: human actions are observed, and the goal is to infer the motivations behind them in order to predict them in the future.

Backwards approaches Here, state information is available (even if just the end state), and we usually seek to infer the sequence of actions that lead to this state. Theoretically, these approaches call back to earlier domains of modeling: means-ends analysis (Newell and Simon, 1961), backtracking (Golomb and Baumert, 1965) and regression planning (McDermott, 1991; Xu et al., 2019). These methods all assume access to the final state, and use this information to arrive here. We will discuss recent approaches incorporating these ideas into NLP (Gandhi et al., 2024; Chen et al., 2024a). We will also discuss backwards reasoning in terms of latent variable modeling, for example: discovering in-context learning examples (Min et al., 2022); infer underlying topics by generating and clustering language-modeling responses (Pham et al., 2024); learning form and structure via the Bayesian Wake-Sleep algorithm; and infer chain-of-thought reasoning steps through bootstrapping (Zelikman et al., 2022). We will highlight the overlapping symmetry between variational inference formulas and classical RL formulations. By illustrating how latent variable modeling and imitation learning can be integrated to infer and utilize latent plans, we discuss the benefits of combining these approaches for modeling creative tasks.

2.3 Evaluation Methods for Creative Plans

"The unexamined life is not worth living."

Plato, Apology of Socrates

For the majority of tasks in creative domains, there is no objective metric for when a plan is successful: creative tasks can be ill-defined, with multiple alternative plans being equally preferable. Thus, in this section of the tutorial, we will focus on evaluation methods based around human preference. There are two modes of evaluation:

Offline Evaluation In this evaluation setting, we assume that we cannot conduct human experiments on enough subjects to make meaningful conclusions, either because they are unavailable or too expensive to obtain data from. The goal of evaluations in this setting is to compare *our* plans to what human plans *would have been*. Novel metrics that have emerged in this space and have been used to evaluate planning include: *latent criticism* (Shi et al., 2023) and *conditional perplexity* (Chen et al., 2019). Latent criticism involves modeling and evaluating the underlying reasoning processes in language models, while conditional perplexity assesses the alignment between generated text and the intended plan. These evaluation metrics moves beyond surface-level metrics, e.g. BLEU or ROUGE scores, whose limitations we will discuss, towards structural comparisons of the output. They are appealing because they allow us to validate in a largely offline manner, without recruiting subject participants.

Online Evaluation Evaluation methods in this setting fall more into a Human-Computer Interaction (HCI) framework of evaluation. In this setting, subject participants are recruited and either asked to conduct trials or are allowed to use tools and then observed. HCI approaches to studying human preferences for plans can involve studying human preferences for recommendations (Spangher, 2015; Zhao et al., 2023), suggestions (Clark and Smith, 2021), edits (Laban et al., 2024) and other aides that a model can provide short of generating an entire text. We will not focus too deeply on this area, though, at the risk of being duplicative with other tutorials.

3 Data Regimes: Full, Partial and Low

In order to conceptualize methods required to study creative planning, we divide creative tasks into three categories based on the availability of data: **Full Visibility**, **Partial Visibility** and **Low Visibility**. To frame these categories, we use vocabulary from the field of reinforcement learning: *actions* refers to planning steps or inferences the model can take. *State-space* refers broadly to textual states (e.g. utterances, documents or retrievals) that are caused or influenced by actions.

Low Data Regimens: settings in which little-to-no data is available about the planning process, including either the end-states or any of the actions or states in between. Examples of tasks in this domain, including: OSWorld (Xie et al., 2024b), WebArena (Zhou et al., 2023) and other web-agent tasks (Branavan et al., 2009; Shi et al., 2017; Liu et al., 2018; Deng et al., 2023; Kim et al., 2024; Gur et al.), where the language model is tasked with navigating webpages without any examples of the output.

Partial Data Regiments: settings where end-state information, but no actions, are available to the planning process. Tasks in this planning domain encompass fields like: computational journalism (Spangher et al., 2024a), computational law (Ravichander et al., 2019), scientific writing (Si et al., 2024) and creative fictional writing (Huang et al., 2023; Tian et al., 2024a). In these tasks, it is typically cheap to collect voluminous datasets of finished news articles, for instance, but it is typically too expensive to observe actions leading up to the finished articles.

Partial-to-Full Data Regiments are characterized by situations in which pre-final text *and/or* action sequences are available for the models to train on. We briefly introduce various tasks and domains where datasets have emerged to support these plans plans, such as tool learning (Schick et al., 2023; Patil et al., 2023; Qin et al., 2023; Li et al., 2023), edit prediction (Spangher et al., 2022b; Lee et al., 2024), math problem-solving (Cobbe et al., 2021; Hendrycks et al., 2021) and instruction-learning (Wu et al., 2023, 2022). In these settings, more of a supervised approach can be taken to learn plans.

4 Application Domains of Creative Planning: Demonstrations

Having established a better definition for "plans" and methods for inferring plans from observed text, we close by discussing applications in various domains. We will give live demonstration of creative tools and compare tools that do not formally plan (e.g. those that engineer sequences of prompts) with tools that do.

Computational Journalism (CJ) This field aims to build decision-support tools for journalists to help find stories and sources; verifying facts; and write articles (Cohen et al., 2011). CJ gives us a good example of a domain of tasks where (1) abundant medium-visibility data exists (2) professional standards across organizations dictate regular and formalized planning and (3) outcomes are socially beneficial. Recent tasks in CJ include: "help a journalist find informational sources to support the story" (Huang et al., 2024a; Spangher et al., a,b; Lu et al.), "find newsworthy stories to cover" (Spangher et al., 2024b; Welsh et al.; Diakopoulos et al., 2010), "plan longer-term article structures" (Spangher et al., 2022a, 2021; Choubey et al., 2020). We will showcase tools without formalized planning, such as *AngleKindling*, a tool for angle selection in journalistic writing (Petridis et al., 2023). We then demonstrate tools that learn and utilize latent plans to enhance output quality, such as *NewsSources* (Huang et al., 2024a) and SPINACH (Liu et al., 2024).

Proactive Task-oriented Agents This field aims to build agents to proactively identify and clarify missing or ambiguous information essential to methodical, domain-specific tasks (Lu et al.; Wu et al., 2025; Liu et al., 2025). By systematically examining the effects of partially available information, these methods train models to optimally balance the cost of queries against the improved accuracy and completeness of their outputs. This proactive reasoning capability significantly enhances the practical utility, creativity and reliability of task-oriented agents, particularly in high-stakes, information-sensitive environments, and represents a promising direction for human–AI collaborative systems.

Creative Writing and Editing Planning plays a crucial role in creative language generation, especially in long-form text generation. Content planning, such as sketching out plot points (Yao et al., 2019; Ammanabrolu et al., 2020; Clark and Smith, 2021), has been shown to improve the quality of generated stories and for generating creative outputs like poetry, where form constraints must be adhered to (Tian and Peng, 2022), or metaphor or figurative language (Chakrabarty et al., 2021) must be used. Incorporating knowledge into the planning process can significantly enhance the ability of LLMs to produce more nuanced, creative outputs (Bosselut et al., 2019; Chakrabarty et al., 2024).

5 Broader Relevance: Connection to Existing Fields

We situate creative planning in a broader field of artificial intelligence and natural language processing, with explicit intersections in:

- **Creative Generation**: Although recent tutorials (Chakrabarty et al., 2023) have covered creative generation, prior work has focused more on the "final product" of generation (e.g. longer-form structural output, cohesiveness and evaluation), not the planning steps. However, awareness of creative processes in different fields and the ability of LLMs to understand and use plans have progressed rapidly, necessitating a novel iteration to explicitly focus on planning in creative tasks.
- **Agentic Planning**: Task-oriented planning (Yu et al., 2023; Huang et al., 2024b; Deng et al., 2024; Zhang et al., 2024; Kohli and Sun, 2024; Xie et al., 2024a), agentic workflows (Wang et al., 2023, 2024; Sodhi et al., 2024; Huang et al., 2024c, 2025) likewise is an area that has received tremendous interest. However, we find the focus of planning in *creative* tasks to be notably lacking. As we will show, creative tasks are tantalizing tasks for planners and agents because trajectories must be

developed on the fly in these domains (Côté et al., 2018; Shridhar et al., 2020, 2021; Tian et al., 2024b).

- **Human-Centered NLP**: A large emphasis in prior Human-Centered NLP tutorials (Yang et al., 2024) has been in Human-Computer Interaction (HCI)-focused methodologies. While this is an important component, we will explicitly focus on emerging experimental methodologies that seek to *infer* human preferences in approaches that can often be more generalizable and robust than direct observational studies.

We consider the following skills useful for researchers considering making advances in creative planning:

- **Latent Variable Modeling**: an understanding of classical Bayesian graphical modeling and hierarchical reasoning. Understand how reinforcement learning, specifically imitation learning, forms the basis for human preference learning.

- **Evaluation Methods for Latent Plans**: Evaluation metrics, like latent evaluation techniques like latent criticism and conditional perplexity, that go beyond surface-level assessments.

- **Creative Agentic Workflows**: Explore how inferred plans are applied in creative tasks. Analyze the differences in model performance when optimizing for concrete rewards versus abstract, creative goals (i.e. imitating human preference). Demonstrate of creative tools and compare those that use engineered prompt sequences with those that utilize latent plans.

6 Suggested Reading List Summary

This tutorial will include our own work, notably in the fields of computational journalism, creativity, latent variable modeling and agent modeling (Huang et al., 2024a; Spangher et al., 2024a, b; Welsh et al.; Spangher et al., 2021; Lu et al.; Tian et al., 2024b) and work by other researchers in NLP and machine learning communities, including but not limited to: (Petridis et al., 2023; Shi et al., 2023; Deng et al., 2023; Schick et al., 2023; Shridhar et al., 2020; Chakrabarty et al., 2023; Zelikman et al., 2022).

7 Tutorial Instructors

Our instructors consist of experts who have conducted research in different aspects related to this tutorial topic.

Alexander Spangher Alexander Spangher is a final-year Ph.D. Candidate in the Department of Computer Science at University of Southern California. He is the recipient of a Bloomberg PhD fellowship and an Outstanding Paper awards at EMNLP 2024 and NAACL 2022. His research focuses on planning, with specific applications in Computational Journalism, law and music. Prior to this, he was a data journalist at *The New York Times*.

Tenghao Huang Tenghao Huang is a Ph.D. Candidate in the Department of Computer Science at University of Southern California. Tenghao is a receipt of ISI distinguished graduate researcher fellowship. His research interests lie in agents and information retrieval. His recent work focuses on bridging the gaps between agents and creative tasks through planning and grounding. Prior to this, Tenghao received his bachelor degree from the University of North Carolina at Chapel Hill.

Philippe Laban Philippe Laban is a Research Scientist at Microsoft Research. His research is at the intersection of NLP and HCI, focusing on several tasks within text generation, including text simplification and summarization. He received his Ph.D. in Computer Science from UC Berkeley in 2021. His recent work has focused on expanding the scope of text simplification to the paragraph and document-level and evaluating textediting interfaces.

Nanyun (Violet) Peng Nanyun (Violet) Peng is an Assistant Professor in the Department of Computer Science at the University of California Los Angeles. She received her Ph.D. in Computer Science from Johns Hopkins University. Her research focuses on the generalizability of NLP technologies, with applications to creative language generation, low-resource information extraction, and zero-shot cross-lingual transfer. Her works have won the Outstanding Paper Award at NAACL 2022, the Best Paper Award at AAAI 2022 Deep Learning on Graphs workshop, and have been featured an IJCAI 2022 early career spotlight.

References

Pieter Abbeel and Andrew Y Ng. 2004. Apprenticeship learning via inverse reinforcement learning. In *Proceedings of the twenty-first international conference on Machine learning*, page 1.

Prithviraj Ammanabrolu, Wesley Cheung, Anju Dhamala Dang, William Broniec, Matthew Hausknecht, and Mark O. Riedl. 2020. Story realization: Expanding plot events into sentences. In *Proceedings of the 2020 Conference on Empirical Methods in Natural Language Processing (EMNLP)*, pages 9055–9069.

Antoine Bosselut, Hannah Rashkin, Maarten Sap, Chaitanya Malaviya, Asli Celikyilmaz, and Yejin Choi. 2019. Comet: Commonsense transformers for automatic knowledge graph construction. In *Proceedings of the 57th Annual Meeting of the Association for Computational Linguistics*, pages 4762–4779.

S.R.K. Branavan, Harr Chen, Luke Zettlemoyer, and Regina Barzilay. 2009. Reinforcement learning for mapping instructions to actions. In *Proceedings of the Joint Conference of the 47th Annual Meeting of the ACL and the 4th International Joint Conference on Natural Language Processing of the AFNLP*, pages 82–90, Suntec, Singapore. Association for Computational Linguistics.

Tuhin Chakrabarty, Philippe Laban, Divyansh Agarwal, Smaranda Muresan, and Chien-Sheng Wu. 2021. Mermaid: Metaphor generation with symbolism and discriminative decoding. In *Proceedings of the 2021 Conference of the North American Chapter of the Association for Computational Linguistics: Human Language Technologies*, pages 4250–4261.

Tuhin Chakrabarty, Philippe Laban, and Chien-Sheng Wu. 2024. Can ai writing be salvaged? mitigating idiosyncrasies and improving human-ai alignment in the writing process through edits. *arXiv preprint arXiv:2409.14509*.

Tuhin Chakrabarty, Vishakh Padmakumar, He He, and Nanyun Peng. 2023. Creative natural language generation. In *Proceedings of the 2023 Conference on Empirical Methods in Natural Language Processing: Tutorial Abstracts*, pages 34–40, Singapore. Association for Computational Linguistics.

Justin Chih-Yao Chen, Zifeng Wang, Hamid Palangi, Rujun Han, Sayna Ebrahimi, Long Le, Vincent Perot, Swaroop Mishra, Mohit Bansal, Chen-Yu Lee, et al. 2024a. Reverse thinking makes llms stronger reasoners. *arXiv preprint arXiv:2411.19865*.

Xinyun Chen, Changliu Wang, Fisher Yu, and Dawn Song. 2019. Evaluating the factual consistency of abstractive text summarization. *arXiv preprint arXiv:1909.12840*.

Zixiang Chen, Yihe Deng, Huizhuo Yuan, Kaixuan Ji, and Quanquan Gu. 2024b. Self-play fine-tuning converts weak language models to strong language models. *Preprint*, arXiv:2401.01335.

Prafulla Kumar Choubey, Aaron Lee, Ruihong Huang, and Lu Wang. 2020. Discourse as a function of event: Profiling discourse structure in news articles around the main event. In *Proceedings of the 58th Annual Meeting of the Association for Computational Linguistics*.

Elizabeth Clark and Noah A Smith. 2021. Choose your own adventure: Paired suggestions in collaborative writing for evaluating story generation models. In *Proceedings of the 2021 Conference of the North American Chapter of the Association for Computational Linguistics: Human Language Technologies*, pages 3566–3575.

Karl Cobbe, Vineet Kosaraju, Mohammad Bavarian, Jacob Hilton, Reiichiro Nakano, and John Schulman. 2021. Training verifiers to solve math word problems. *arXiv preprint arXiv:2110.14168*.

Sarah Cohen, James T Hamilton, and Fred Turner. 2011. Computational journalism. *Communications of the ACM*, 54(10):66–71.

Marc-Alexandre Côté, Ákos Kádár, Xingdi Yuan, Ben Kybartas, Tavian Barnes, Emery Fine, James Moore, Matthew Hausknecht, Layla El Asri, Mahmoud Adada, et al. 2018. Textworld: A learning environment for text-based games. In *Workshop on Computer Games*, pages 41–75. Springer.

Edward de Bono. 1992. *Serious Creativity: Using the Power of Lateral Thinking to Create New Ideas*. HarperBusiness.

Xiang Deng, Yu Gu, Boyuan Zheng, Shijie Chen, Sam Stevens, Boshi Wang, Huan Sun, and Yu Su. 2024. Mind2web: Towards a generalist agent for the web. *Advances in Neural Information Processing Systems*, 36.

Xiang Deng, Yu Gu, Boyuan Zheng, Shijie Chen, Samuel Stevens, Boshi Wang, Huan Sun, and Yu Su. 2023. Mind2web: Towards a generalist agent for the web. *Preprint*, arXiv:2306.06070.

Nicholas Diakopoulos, Mor Naaman, and Funda Kivran-Swaine. 2010. Diamonds in the rough: Social media visual analytics for journalistic inquiry. In *2010 IEEE Symposium on Visual Analytics Science and Technology*, pages 115–122. IEEE.

Albert Einstein and Leopold Infeld. 1938. *The Evolution of Physics*. Simon and Schuster, New York.

Ronald A Finke. 1996. Imagery, creativity, and emergent structure. *Consciousness and cognition*, 5(3):381–393.

Kanishk Gandhi, Denise Lee, Gabriel Grand, Muxin Liu, Winson Cheng, Archit Sharma, and Noah D Goodman. 2024. Stream of search (sos): Learning to search in language. *arXiv preprint arXiv:2404.03683*.

Dedre Gentner and Phillip Wolff. 2014. Metaphor and knowledge change. In *Cognitive dynamics*, pages 295–342. Psychology Press.

Jacob W Getzels and Mihaly Csikszentmihalyi. 1976. The creative vision: A longitudinal study of problem finding in art.

Solomon W Golomb and Leonard D Baumert. 1965. Backtrack programming. *Journal of the ACM (JACM)*, 12(4):516–524.

Joy Paul Guilford. 1950. Creativity. *American psychologist*, 5(9):444–454.

Joy Paul Guilford, Paul R Christensen, Philip R Merrifield, and Robert C Wilson. 1978. Alternate uses.

Izzeddin Gur, Hiroki Furuta, Austin V Huang, Mustafa Safdari, Yutaka Matsuo, Douglas Eck, and Aleksandra Faust. A real-world webagent with planning, long context understanding, and program synthesis. In *The Twelfth International Conference on Learning Representations*.

Dan Hendrycks, Collin Burns, Saurav Kadavath, Akul Arora, Steven Basart, Andy Zou, Mantas Mazeika, Dawn Song, and Jacob Steinhardt. 2021. Measuring mathematical problem solving with the math dataset. *arXiv preprint arXiv:2103.03874*.

Lydia M Hopper. 2010. 'ghost'experiments and the dissection of social learning in humans and animals. *Biological Reviews*, 85(4):685–701.

Tenghao Huang, Kinjal Basu, Ibrahim Abdelaziz, Pavan Kapanipathi, Jonathan May, and Muhao Chen. 2025. R2d2: Remembering, reflecting and dynamic decision making for web agents. *Preprint*, arXiv:2501.12485.

Tenghao Huang, Yiqin Huang, Lucas Spangher, Sewon Min, Mark Dredze, and Alexander Spangher. 2024a. A novel multi-document retrieval benchmark grounded on journalist source-selection in newswriting.

Tenghao Huang, Dongwon Jung, Vaibhav Kumar, Mohammad Kachuee, Xiang Li, Puyang Xu, and Muhao Chen. 2024b. Planning and editing what you retrieve for enhanced tool learning. In *Findings of the Association for Computational Linguistics: NAACL 2024*, pages 975–988, Mexico City, Mexico. Association for Computational Linguistics.

Tenghao Huang, Donghee Lee, John Sweeney, Jiatong Shi, Emily Steliotes, Matthew Lange, Jonathan May, and Muhao Chen. 2024c. Foodpuzzle: Developing large language model agents as flavor scientists. *Preprint*, arXiv:2409.12832.

Tenghao Huang, Ehsan Qasemi, Bangzheng Li, He Wang, Faeze Brahman, Muhao Chen, and Snigdha Chaturvedi. 2023. Affective and dynamic beam search for story generation. *Findings of the Association for Computational Linguistics: EMNLP 2023*.

Geunwoo Kim, Pierre Baldi, and Stephen McAleer. 2024. Language models can solve computer tasks. *Advances in Neural Information Processing Systems*, 36.

Harsh Kohli and Huan Sun. 2024. Cleared for takeoff? compositional conditional reasoning may be the achilles heel to (flight-booking) language agents. *Preprint*, arXiv:2404.04237.

Philippe Laban, Jesse Vig, Marti Hearst, Caiming Xiong, and Chien-Sheng Wu. 2024. Beyond the chat: Executable and verifiable text-editing with llms. In *Proceedings of the 37th Annual ACM Symposium on User Interface Software and Technology*, pages 1–23.

Ryan Lee, Alexander Spangher, and Xuezhe Ma. 2024. Patentedits: Framing patent novelty as textual entailment.

Minghao Li, Yingxiu Zhao, Bowen Yu, Feifan Song, Hangyu Li, Haiyang Yu, Zhoujun Li, Fei Huang, and Yongbin Li. 2023. Api-bank: A comprehensive benchmark for tool-augmented llms. *Preprint*, arXiv:2304.08244.

Evan Zheran Liu, Kelvin Guu, Panupong Pasupat, and Percy Liang. 2018. Reinforcement learning on web interfaces using workflow-guided exploration. In *International Conference on Learning Representations*.

Shicheng Liu, Sina J Semnani, Harold Triedman, Jialiang Xu, Isaac Dan Zhao, and Monica S Lam. 2024. Spinach: Sparql-based information navigation for challenging real-world questions. *arXiv preprint arXiv:2407.11417*.

Xingyu Bruce Liu, Shitao Fang, Weiyan Shi, Chien-Sheng Wu, Takeo Igarashi, and Xiang Anthony Chen. 2025. Proactive conversational agents with inner thoughts. *Preprint*, arXiv:2501.00383.

Michael Lu, Hyundong Cho, Weiyan Shi, Jonathan May, and Alexander Spangher. Newsinterview: a dataset and a playground to evaluate llms' ground gap via informational interviews.

Drew McDermott. 1991. Regression planning. *International Journal of Intelligent Systems*, 6(4):357–416.

Sewon Min, Mike Lewis, Hannaneh Hajishirzi, and Luke Zettlemoyer. 2022. Rethinking the role of demonstrations: What makes in-context learning work? *arXiv preprint arXiv:2202.12837*.

Allen Newell and Herbert Alexander Simon. 1961. Gps, a program that simulates human thought.

Shishir G Patil, Tianjun Zhang, Xin Wang, and Joseph E Gonzalez. 2023. Gorilla: Large language model connected with massive apis. *arXiv preprint arXiv:2305.15334*.

Savvas Petridis, Nicholas Diakopoulos, Kevin Crowston, Mark Hansen, Keren Henderson, Stan Jastrzebski, Jeffrey V Nickerson, and Lydia B Chilton. 2023.

Anglekindling: Supporting journalistic angle ideation with large language models. In *Proceedings of the 2023 CHI conference on human factors in computing systems*, pages 1–16.

Chau Pham, Alexander Hoyle, Simeng Sun, Philip Resnik, and Mohit Iyyer. 2024. Topicgpt: A prompt-based topic modeling framework. In *Proceedings of the 2024 Conference of the North American Chapter of the Association for Computational Linguistics: Human Language Technologies (Volume 1: Long Papers)*, pages 2956–2984.

Yujia Qin, Shihao Liang, Yining Ye, Kunlun Zhu, Lan Yan, Yaxi Lu, Yankai Lin, Xin Cong, Xiangru Tang, Bill Qian, et al. 2023. Toolllm: Facilitating large language models to master 16000+ real-world apis. *arXiv preprint arXiv:2307.16789*.

Abhilasha Ravichander, Alan W Black, Shomir Wilson, Thomas Norton, and Norman Sadeh. 2019. Question answering for privacy policies: Combining computational and legal perspectives. In *Proceedings of the 2019 Conference on Empirical Methods in Natural Language Processing and the 9th International Joint Conference on Natural Language Processing (EMNLP-IJCNLP)*, pages 4947–4958, Hong Kong, China. Association for Computational Linguistics.

Mark A Runco. 2001. Introduction to the special issue: Commemorating guilford's 1950 presidential address. *Creativity Research Journal*, 13(3-4):245–245.

Timo Schick, Jane Dwivedi-Yu, Roberto Dessì, Roberta Raileanu, Maria Lomeli, Luke Zettlemoyer, Nicola Cancedda, and Thomas Scialom. 2023. Toolformer: Language models can teach themselves to use tools. *arXiv preprint arXiv:2302.04761*.

Ruizhe Shi, Yifang Chen, Yushi Hu, Alisa Liu, Hanna Hajishirzi, Noah A Smith, and Simon S Du. 2024. Decoding-time language model alignment with multiple objectives. *Advances in Neural Information Processing Systems*, 37:48875–48920.

Tianlin Shi, Andrej Karpathy, Linxi Fan, Jonathan Hernandez, and Percy Liang. 2017. World of bits: An open-domain platform for web-based agents. In *Proceedings of the 34th International Conference on Machine Learning*, volume 70 of *Proceedings of Machine Learning Research*, pages 3135–3144. PMLR.

Zewei Shi, Wanyu Du, and James Zou. 2023. Large language models as optimizers. *arXiv preprint arXiv:2301.07085*.

Mohit Shridhar, Jesse Thomason, Daniel Gordon, Yonatan Bisk, Winson Han, Roozbeh Mottaghi, Luke Zettlemoyer, and Dieter Fox. 2020. ALFRED: A Benchmark for Interpreting Grounded Instructions for Everyday Tasks. In *The IEEE Conference on Computer Vision and Pattern Recognition (CVPR)*.

Mohit Shridhar, Xingdi Yuan, Marc-Alexandre Côté, Yonatan Bisk, Adam Trischler, and Matthew Hausknecht. 2021. ALFWorld: Aligning Text and Embodied Environments for Interactive Learning. In *Proceedings of the International Conference on Learning Representations (ICLR)*.

Chenglei Si, Diyi Yang, and Tatsunori Hashimoto. 2024. Can llms generate novel research ideas? a large-scale human study with 100+ nlp researchers. *Preprint*, arXiv:2409.04109.

Paloma Sodhi, S. R. K. Branavan, Yoav Artzi, and Ryan McDonald. 2024. Step: Stacked llm policies for web actions. *Preprint*, arXiv:2310.03720.

Yifan Song, Da Yin, Xiang Yue, Jie Huang, Sujian Li, and Bill Yuchen Lin. 2024. Trial and error: Exploration-based trajectory optimization for llm agents. *Preprint*, arXiv:2403.02502.

Alexander Spangher. 2015. Building the next new york times recommendation engine. *The New York Times*, pages 08–26.

Alexander Spangher, Jonathan May, Sz-Rung Shiang, and Lingjia Deng. 2021. Multitask semi-supervised learning for class-imbalanced discourse classification. In *Proceedings of the 2021 conference on empirical methods in natural language processing*, pages 498–517.

Alexander Spangher, Yao Ming, Xinyu Hua, and Nanyun Peng. 2022a. Sequentially controlled text generation. In *Findings of the Association for Computational Linguistics: EMNLP 2022*, pages 6848–6866.

Alexander Spangher, Nanyun Peng, Emilio Ferrara, and Jonathan May. a. Identifying informational sources in news articles. In *The 2023 Conference on Empirical Methods in Natural Language Processing*.

Alexander Spangher, Nanyun Peng, Sebastian Gehrmann, and Mark Dredze. 2024a. Do llms plan like human writers? comparing journalist coverage of press releases with llms. In *Conference on Empirical Methods in Natural Language Processing*.

Alexander Spangher, Xiang Ren, Jonathan May, and Nanyun Peng. 2022b. Newsedits: A news article revision dataset and a novel document-level reasoning challenge. In *Proceedings of the 2022 Conference of the North American Chapter of the Association for Computational Linguistics: Human Language Technologies*, pages 127–157.

Alexander Spangher, Serdar Tumgoren, Ben Welsh, Nanyun Peng, Emilio Ferrara, and Jonathan May. 2024b. Tracking the newsworthiness of public documents. In *Proceedings of the 62nd Annual Meeting of the Association for Computational Linguistics (Volume 1: Long Papers)*, pages 14150–14168, Bangkok, Thailand. Association for Computational Linguistics.

Alexander Spangher, James Youn, Matt DeButts, Nanyun Peng, Emilio Ferrara, and Jonathan May. b. Explaining mixtures of sources in news articles. In *The 2024 Conference on Empirical Methods in Natural Language Processing*.

Giulio Starace, Oliver Jaffe, Dane Sherburn, James Aung, Jun Shern Chan, Leon Maksin, Rachel Dias, Evan Mays, Benjamin Kinsella, Wyatt Thompson, et al. 2025. Paperbench: Evaluating ai's ability to replicate ai research. *arXiv preprint arXiv:2504.01848*.

Yufei Tian, Tenghao Huang, Miri Liu, Derek Jiang, Alexander Spangher, Muhao Chen, Jonathan May, and Nanyun Peng. 2024a. Are large language models capable of generating human-level narratives? *arXiv preprint arXiv:2407.13248*.

Yufei Tian and Nanyun Peng. 2022. Zero-shot sonnet generation with discourse-level planning and aesthetics features. In *Proceedings of the 2022 Conference of the North American Chapter of the Association for Computational Linguistics: Human Language Technologies*, pages 3587–3597.

Yufei Tian, Abhilasha Ravichander, Lianhui Qin, Ronan Le Bras, Raja Marjieh, Nanyun Peng, Yejin Choi, Thomas L. Griffiths, and Faeze Brahman. 2024b. Macgyver: Are large language models creative problem solvers? In *Proceedings of NAACL*.

Zihao Wang, Shaofei Cai, Anji Liu, Xiaojian Ma, and Yitao Liang. 2023. Jarvis-1: Open-world multitask agents with memory-augmented multimodal language models. In *Second Agent Learning in Open-Endedness Workshop*.

Zora Zhiruo Wang, Jiayuan Mao, Daniel Fried, and Graham Neubig. 2024. Agent workflow memory. *arXiv preprint arXiv:2409.07429*.

Benjamin Welsh, Arda Kaz, Michael Vu, Naitian Zhou, and Alexander Spangher. Newshomepages: Homepage layouts capture information prioritization decisions.

Shirley Wu, Michel Galley, Baolin Peng, Hao Cheng, Gavin Li, Yao Dou, Weixin Cai, James Zou, Jure Leskovec, and Jianfeng Gao. 2025. Collabllm: From passive responders to active collaborators. *Preprint*, arXiv:2502.00640.

Te-Lin Wu, Alex Spangher, Pegah Alipoormolabashi, Marjorie Freedman, Ralph Weischedel, and Nanyun Peng. 2022. Understanding multimodal procedural knowledge by sequencing multimodal instructional manuals. In *Proceedings of the 60th Annual Meeting of the Association for Computational Linguistics (Volume 1: Long Papers)*, pages 4525–4542.

Te-Lin Wu, Caiqi Zhang, Qingyuan Hu, Alexander Spangher, and Nanyun Peng. 2023. Learning action conditions from instructional manuals for instruction understanding. In *Proceedings of the 61st Annual Meeting of the Association for Computational Linguistics (Volume 1: Long Papers)*, pages 3023–3043.

Markus Wulfmeier, Michael Bloesch, Nino Vieillard, Arun Ahuja, Jorg Bornschein, Sandy Huang, Artem Sokolov, Matt Barnes, Guillaume Desjardins, Alex Bewley, et al. 2024. Imitating language via scalable inverse reinforcement learning. *Advances in Neural Information Processing Systems*, 37:90714–90735.

Jian Xie, Kai Zhang, Jiangjie Chen, Tinghui Zhu, Renze Lou, Yuandong Tian, Yanghua Xiao, and Yu Su. 2024a. Travelplanner: A benchmark for real-world planning with language agents. In *Forty-first International Conference on Machine Learning*.

Tianbao Xie, Danyang Zhang, Jixuan Chen, Xiaochuan Li, Siheng Zhao, Ruisheng Cao, Toh Jing Hua, Zhoujun Cheng, Dongchan Shin, Fangyu Lei, Yitao Liu, Yiheng Xu, Shuyan Zhou, Silvio Savarese, Caiming Xiong, Victor Zhong, and Tao Yu. 2024b. Osworld: Benchmarking multimodal agents for open-ended tasks in real computer environments. *Preprint*, arXiv:2404.07972.

Danfei Xu, Roberto Martín-Martín, De-An Huang, Yuke Zhu, Silvio Savarese, and Li F Fei-Fei. 2019. Regression planning networks. *Advances in neural information processing systems*, 32.

Diyi Yang, Sherry Tongshuang Wu, and Marti A. Hearst. 2024. Human-AI interaction in the age of LLMs. In *Proceedings of the 2024 Conference of the North American Chapter of the Association for Computational Linguistics: Human Language Technologies (Volume 5: Tutorial Abstracts)*, pages 34–38, Mexico City, Mexico. Association for Computational Linguistics.

Lili Yao, Nanyun Peng, Ralph Weischedel, Kevin Knight, Dongyan Zhao, and Rui Yan. 2019. Plan-and-write: Towards better automatic storytelling. In *Proceedings of the AAAI Conference on Artificial Intelligence*, volume 33, pages 7378–7385.

Xiao Yu, Maximillian Chen, and Zhou Yu. 2023. Prompt-based Monte-Carlo tree search for goal-oriented dialogue policy planning. In *Proceedings of the 2023 Conference on Empirical Methods in Natural Language Processing*, pages 7101–7125, Singapore. Association for Computational Linguistics.

Eric Zelikman, Yuhuai Wu, and Noah D. Goodman. 2022. Star: Bootstrapping reasoning with reasoning in language models. *arXiv preprint arXiv:2203.14465*.

Kexun Zhang, Weiran Yao, Zuxin Liu, Yihao Feng, Zhiwei Liu, Rithesh Murthy, Tian Lan, Lei Li, Renze Lou, Jiacheng Xu, et al. 2024. Diversity empowers intelligence: Integrating expertise of software engineering agents. *arXiv preprint arXiv:2408.07060*.

Zihuai Zhao, Wenqi Fan, Jiatong Li, Yunqing Liu, Xiaowei Mei, Yiqi Wang, Zhen Wen, Fei Wang, Xiangyu Zhao, Jiliang Tang, et al. 2023. Recommender systems in the era of large language models (llms). *arXiv preprint arXiv:2307.02046*.

Shuyan Zhou, Frank F Xu, Hao Zhu, Xuhui Zhou, Robert Lo, Abishek Sridhar, Xianyi Cheng, Yonatan Bisk, Daniel Fried, Uri Alon, et al. 2023. Webarena: A realistic web environment for building autonomous agents. *arXiv preprint arXiv:2307.13854*.

DAMAGeR: Deploying Automatic and Manual Approaches to GenAI Red-teaming

Manish Nagireddy
IBM Research
manish.nagireddy@ibm.com

Michael Feffer
Carnegie Mellon University
mfeffer@andrew.cmu.edu

Ioana Baldini
Bloomberg
ioana.baldini@gmail.com

1 General Information

Title: DAMAGeR: Deploying Automatic and Manual Approaches to GenAI Red-teaming

Type: cutting-edge in CL / NLP

Sub-Areas: Natural Language Processing, Large Language Models, safety and trustworthiness, red-teaming

Presenters:

- Manish Nagireddy, IBM Research, manish.nagireddy@ibm.com
- Michael Feffer, Carnegie Mellon University, mfeffer@andrew.cmu.edu
- Ioana Baldini, Bloomberg, ioana.baldini@gmail.com

Duration: Half day (3 hours plus 30-minute break)

Brief Description: In this tutorial, we will review and apply current automatic and manual red-teaming techniques for GenAI models (including LLMs and multimodal models). In doing so, we aim to emphasize the importance of using a mixture of techniques and establishing a balance between automatic and manual approaches. Lastly, we aim to engage tutorial participants in live red-teaming activities to collaboratively learn impactful red-teaming strategies and share insights.

2 Tutorial Details

2.1 Context

Tools: We will be using the Chatbot Arena (available at https://lmarena.ai/) for all participant interaction with LLMs. As such, audience members will only need a computer with internet access to participate in the live red-teaming session.

History: We led two previous iterations of this interactive exercise. The first was at KDD 2024 (Nagireddy et al., 2024b) with around 30-40 participants. The website and slides used for this event can be found at https://sites.google.com/view/kdd24-red-teaming-tutorial. The second was at AAAI '25, with resources available at https://sites.google.com/view/aaai25red-teaming-tutorial.

We are happy to report that crowd engagement was the highlight of both events.

Estimated Number of Participants: 30-50

Prerequisite Knowledge: Our intended audience is anyone who has an interest in GenAI, with a particular emphasis on potential usage risks. As such, previous interactions with GenAI may be helpful but are not necessary.

2.2 Content

Over the past couple of years, GenAI models with billions of parameters have become readily available to the general public. In turn, a mixture of tangible results and hype has led to eagerness from the public to use GenAI in many different ways. At the same time, there are various concerns surrounding these models, leading to burgeoning efforts to document and classify their negative impacts. Red-teaming, which typically takes the form of interactive probing, is commonly used as part of these efforts. In order to most effectively uncover potential risks via red-teaming, we strongly believe that a participatory effort is paramount. In particular, with this tutorial, we seek to leverage the diverse set of skills and background experiences of conference attendees in order to discover GenAI failures. By providing attendees with varying familiarity with GenAI models and issues with an opportunity to actively red-team generative AI models, we hope to affirm the notion that effective red-teaming requires broad participation and effort. We are confident that our tutorial will encourage attendees

Proceedings of the 2025 Annual Conference of the Nations of the Americas Chapter of the Association for Computational Linguistics: Human Language Technologies: Tutorial Abstracts, pages 10–14

to continue to provide invaluable feedback on the failure modes of these pervasive GenAI models.

The tutorial is split in two parts. The first part has an educational setup, covering important topics in responsible AI and red-teaming. The second part of the tutorial is structured as an interactive exercise, where the audience is engaged in a live red-teaming session. The interactive exercise is performed in several rounds. After each round, the audience engages in a discussion around the most efficient techniques for red-teaming and the topics that seem to exhibit undesirable behavior.

The educational part of the tutorial covers topics such as the advancement of GenAI models and their risks, taxonomies of risks and harms, best practices in participatory red-teaming events. Significant attention is dedicated to red-teaming approaches, in which several tactics and strategies are covered.

The following outlines the structure of the tutorial, along with the papers relevant to each topic.

Part I: Red Teaming 101 (1.5h)

- **Why Red Teaming?**
  - The strengths, benefits, and dangers of LLMs (Bowman, 2022; Weidinger et al., 2023)
  - Risks from generative output (IBM, 2024; Gautam et al., 2024; Weidinger et al., 2022)
  - Red-teaming: Uncovering harmful content through interactive probing (Ganguli et al., 2022; Lin et al., 2024)
- **Participatory Red-teaming**
  - DefCon31: Generative AI Red-teaming Challenge (Intelligence et al., 2024; White House, 2023)
  - Red-teaming LLMs for resilience to scientific disinformation (The Royal Society and Humane Intelligence, 2024)
  - AdversarialNibbler (Quaye et al., 2024)
- **State-of-the-art in Red-teaming Research**
  - Attack strategies: affirmative completion (Wei et al., 2023), context switching (Schulhoff et al., 2023), contextual interaction attack (Cheng et al., 2024), instruction indirection (Jiang et al., 2024), ciphers (Yuan et al., 2024), role play (Shah et al., 2023) and persuasion (Zeng et al., 2024)
  - Automatic/AI-based approaches (Kour et al., 2023; Hong et al., 2024; Perez et al., 2022; Radharapu et al., 2023; Mazeika et al., 2024; Casper et al., 2023)
  - Red-teaming Multi-modal LMs (Quaye et al., 2024; Luccioni et al., 2023; Mahato et al., 2024)
  - Red-teaming tooling (Derczynski et al., 2024; Microsoft, 2024; Mazeika et al., 2024; Chiang et al., 2024)

Part II: Hands-on LLM Red Teaming (1h): A live, interactive red-teaming session where participants use the insights learned from Part I of the tutorial in order to elicit model failures.

- Round 1: Paired unrestricted red-teaming + Full Discussion
- Round 2: Paired and risk specific red-teaming + Full Discussion
- Final Round: Larger Group free range red-teaming + Full Discussion
- Final Recap Discussion

Part III: What Red-Teaming Cannot Address (0.5h):

- AI Red-Teaming Is Not a One-Stop Solution to AI Harms
- Algorithmic monoculture and social welfare (Kleinberg and Raghavan, 2021)

3 Reading List

We do not require attendees to read specific works as the first half of the tutorial will review pertinent literature. For those who wish to be familiar with various red-teaming aspects prior to the start of the event, we have provided the list of recommended works to study below:

- Perez et al. (2022) "Red-teaming Language Models with Language Models"
- Ganguli et al. (2022) "Red-teaming Language Models to Reduce Harms"
- Zou et al. (2023) "Universal and Transferable Adversarial Attacks on Aligned Language Models"
- Wei et al. (2023) "Jailbroken: How Does LLM Safety Training Fail?"

- Feffer et al. (2024) "Red-Teaming for Generative AI: Silver Bullet or Security Theater?"
- Lin et al. (2024) "Against The Achilles' Heel: A Survey on Red Teaming for Generative Models"

4 Diversity and Inclusion

We perceive red-teaming as an exercise that is best conducted with a diverse crowd. As such, we intend to tap into the affinity groups that attend the *ACL conferences, such as Women in NLP, LatinX in AI, Black in AI, and Queer in AI, and encourage them to participate. We believe that researchers with different lived experiences lead to different and effective ways for red-teaming. This is supported by prior work which argues for more stakeholder and marginalized community inclusion upon discovering GenAI issues such as stereotype reinforcement or lack of support for low-resource languages (e.g., (Luccioni et al., 2023; Yong et al., 2023)). Ideally, we could strive to create a community of red-teamers that could meet periodically to conduct virtual red-teaming exercises and write-up our findings. This would be a first step of creating a community that periodically red-teams the latest models. Infrastructure such as Chat Arena (`https://lmarena.ai/`) can facilitate such exercises.

5 Speaker Biographies

Manish Nagireddy is a Research Software Engineer at IBM Research AI and the MIT-IBM Watson AI Lab. His main research goal is to build trustworthy AI solutions. His research interests encompass several areas in machine learning and artificial intelligence from classical ML methods to natural language processing and the generative context. His current work focuses on use-case centered algorithmic auditing and evaluation, in the context of large language models. He has worked on benchmarking large language models for safety (Nagireddy et al., 2024a) as well as building guardrail models for LLMs (Achintalwar et al., 2024; Nagireddy et al., 2024c).

Michael Feffer is a Societal Computing PhD student at Carnegie Mellon University (CMU). His research involves examining the interactions between AI and society. It includes but is not limited to algorithmic fairness, AI for social good, participatory approaches to machine learning, and the ethics and evaluation of generative AI models. Through leveraging both quantitative and qualitative research approaches, he aims to develop frameworks whereby everyday people impacted by ML models can influence model development.

Ioana Baldini is a Generative AI strategist in the CTO office at Bloomberg. Previously, Ioana was a Senior Research Scientist at IBM Research AI, where she focused on social bias auditing and red-teaming of language models. Ioana has a diverse research background, with a proven record in different research areas that span computer architecture, runtime systems, cloud infrastructure and applied natural language processing. She enjoys working in large, multi-disciplinary projects.

6 Other Logistics

- We intend to make all tutorial presentation materials publicly available after the event has concluded. As we did previously, we will create a website and upload the slides used for the event at `https://sites.google.com/view/naacl25red-teaming-tutorial`

7 Ethics Statement

We recognize that participants will be exposed to harmful and dangerous content in both passive and active manners. Before showing any harmful text, we will provide the proper disclaimers and continually let participants know that they may step out at any time if the content is too upsetting. Additionally, when the participants are actively red-teaming the models, we will encourage them to take breaks and understand that they are explicitly trying to elicit harmful outputs. Our cycling of around 15 minutes on and off for active red-teaming is intentional, so as to reduce mental fatigue as well encourage communal dialogue.

References

Swapnaja Achintalwar, Adriana Alvarado Garcia, Ateret Anaby-Tavor, Ioana Baldini, Sara E. Berger, Bishwaranjan Bhattacharjee, Djallel Bouneffouf, Subhajit Chaudhury, Pin-Yu Chen, Lamogha Chiazor, Elizabeth M. Daly, Kirushikesh DB, Rogério Abreu de Paula, Pierre Dognin, Eitan Farchi, Soumya Ghosh, Michael Hind, Raya Horesh, George Kour, Ja Young Lee, Nishtha Madaan, Sameep Mehta, Erik Miehling, Keerthiram Murugesan, Manish Nagireddy, Inkit Padhi, David Piorkowski, Ambrish Rawat, Orna Raz, Prasanna Sattigeri, Hendrik Strobelt, Sarathkrishna Swaminathan, Christoph Tillmann, Aashka Trivedi, Kush R. Varshney, Dennis Wei, Shalisha Witherspooon, and Marcel Zalmanovici. 2024. Detectors for safe and reliable llms: Implementations, uses, and limitations. *Preprint*, arXiv:2403.06009.

Samuel Bowman. 2022. The dangers of underclaiming: Reasons for caution when reporting how NLP systems fail. In *Proceedings of the Annual Meeting of the Association for Computational Linguistics (ACL)*.

Stephen Casper, Jason Lin, Joe Kwon, Gatlen Culp, and Dylan Hadfield-Menell. 2023. Explore, establish, exploit: Red teaming language models from scratch. *Preprint*, arXiv:2306.09442.

Yixin Cheng, Markos Georgopoulos, Volkan Cevher, and Grigorios G. Chrysos. 2024. Leveraging the context through multi-round interactions for jailbreaking attacks. *Preprint*, arXiv:2402.09177.

Wei-Lin Chiang, Lianmin Zheng, Ying Sheng, Anastasios Nikolas Angelopoulos, Tianle Li, Dacheng Li, Hao Zhang, Banghua Zhu, Michael Jordan, Joseph E. Gonzalez, and Ion Stoica. 2024. Chatbot arena: An open platform for evaluating llms by human preference. *Preprint*, arXiv:2403.04132.

Leon Derczynski, Erick Galinkin, and Subho Majumdar. 2024. garak: A Framework for Large Language Model Red Teaming. `https://garak.ai`.

Michael Feffer, Anusha Sinha, Wesley H Deng, Zachary C Lipton, and Hoda Heidari. 2024. Red-teaming for generative ai: Silver bullet or security theater? In *Proceedings of the AAAI/ACM Conference on AI, Ethics, and Society*, volume 7, pages 421–437.

Deep Ganguli, Liane Lovitt, Jackson Kernion, Amanda Askell, Yuntao Bai, Saurav Kadavath, Ben Mann, Ethan Perez, Nicholas Schiefer, Kamal Ndousse, et al. 2022. Red teaming language models to reduce harms: Methods, scaling behaviors, and lessons learned. *CoRR*, abs/2209.07858.

Sanjana Gautam, Pranav Narayanan Venkit, and Sourojit Ghosh. 2024. From melting pots to misrepresentations: Exploring harms in generative ai. In *CHI 2024: Generative AI and HCI workshop*.

Zhang-Wei Hong, Idan Shenfeld, Tsun-Hsuan Wang, Yung-Sung Chuang, Aldo Pareja, James Glass, Akash Srivastava, and Pulkit Agrawal. 2024. Curiosity-driven red-teaming for large language models.

IBM. 2024. Ai risk atlas.

Humane Intelligence, Seed AI, and DefCon AI Village. 2024. Generative ai red teaming challenge: Transparency report. `https://drive.google.com/file/d/1JqpbIP6DNomkb32umLoiEPombK2-0Rc-/view`.

Fengqing Jiang, Zhangchen Xu, Luyao Niu, Zhen Xiang, Bhaskar Ramasubramanian, Bo Li, and Radha Poovendran. 2024. Artprompt: Ascii art-based jailbreak attacks against aligned llms. In *Proceedings of the Annual Meeting of the Association for Computational Linguistics (ACL)*.

Jon Kleinberg and Manish Raghavan. 2021. Algorithmic monoculture and social welfare. *Proceedings of the National Academy of Sciences*, 118(22):e2018340118.

George Kour, Marcel Zalmanovici, Naama Zwerdling, Esther Goldbraich, Ora Nova Fandina, Ateret Anaby-Tavor, Orna Raz, and Eitan Farchi. 2023. Unveiling safety vulnerabilities of large language models. *Preprint*, arXiv:2311.04124.

Lizhi Lin, Honglin Mu, Zenan Zhai, Minghan Wang, Yuxia Wang, Renxi Wang, Junjie Gao, Yixuan Zhang, Wanxiang Che, Timothy Baldwin, Xudong Han, and Haonan Li. 2024. Against the achilles' heel: A survey on red teaming for generative models. *Preprint*, arXiv:2404.00629.

Alexandra Sasha Luccioni, Christopher Akiki, Margaret Mitchell, and Yacine Jernite. 2023. Stable bias: Analyzing societal representations in diffusion models. In *Advances in Neural Information Processing Systems (NeurIPS) Datasets and Benchmarks Track*.

Moushumi Mahato, Avinash Kumar, Kartikey Singh, Bhavesh Kukreja, and Javaid Nabi. 2024. Red teaming for multimodal large language models: A survey.

Mantas Mazeika, Long Phan, Xuwang Yin, Andy Zou, Zifan Wang, Norman Mu, Elham Sakhaee, Nathaniel Li, Steven Basart, Bo Li, et al. 2024. Harmbench: A standardized evaluation framework for automated red teaming and robust refusal. *Preprint*, arXiv:2402.04249.

Microsoft. 2024. Python risk identification tool for generative ai (pyrit).

Manish Nagireddy, Lamogha Chiazor, Moninder Singh, and Ioana Baldini. 2024a. Socialstigmaqa: A benchmark to uncover stigma amplification in generative language models. *Proceedings of the AAAI Conference on Artificial Intelligence*, (19):21454–21462.

Manish Nagireddy, Bernat Guillén Pegueroles, and Ioana Baldini. 2024b. Dare to diversify: Data driven and diverse llm red teaming. In *Proceedings of the 30th ACM SIGKDD Conference on Knowledge Discovery and Data Mining*, KDD '24, page 6420–6421, New York, NY, USA. Association for Computing Machinery.

Manish Nagireddy, Inkit Padhi, Soumya Ghosh, and Prasanna Sattigeri. 2024c. When in doubt, cascade: Towards building efficient and capable guardrails. *Preprint*, arXiv:2407.06323.

Ethan Perez, Saffron Huang, Francis Song, Trevor Cai, Roman Ring, John Aslanides, Amelia Glaese, Nat McAleese, and Geoffrey Irving. 2022. Red teaming language models with language models. In *Proceedings of the Conference on Empirical Methods in Natural Language Processing, EMNLP 2022, Abu Dhabi, United Arab Emirates, December 7-11, 2022*.

Jessica Quaye, Alicia Parrish, Oana Inel, Charvi Rastogi, Hannah Rose Kirk, Minsuk Kahng, Erin Van Liemt, Max Bartolo, Jess Tsang, Justin White, Nathan Clement, Rafael Mosquera, Juan Ciro, Vijay Janapa Reddi, and Lora Aroyo. 2024. Adversarial nibbler: An open red-teaming method for identifying diverse harms in text-to-image generation. In *Proceedings of the ACM Conference on Fairness, Accountability, and Transparency (FAccT)*.

Bhaktipriya Radharapu, Kevin Robinson, Lora Aroyo, and Preethi Lahoti. 2023. AART: AI-assisted red-teaming with diverse data generation for new LLM-powered applications. In *Proceedings of the Conference on Empirical Methods in Natural Language Processing (EMNLP) Industry Track*.

Sander Schulhoff, Jeremy Pinto, Anaum Khan, Louis-François Bouchard, Chenglei Si, Svetlina Anati, Valen Tagliabue, Anson Kost, Christopher Carnahan, and Jordan Boyd-Graber. 2023. Ignore this title and HackAPrompt: Exposing systemic vulnerabilities of LLMs through a global prompt hacking competition. In *Proceedings of the Conference on Empirical Methods in Natural Language Processing (EMNLP)*.

Rusheb Shah, Quentin Feuillade-Montixi, Soroush Pour, Arush Tagade, Stephen Casper, and Javier Rando. 2023. Scalable and transferable black-box jailbreaks for language models via persona modulation. *Preprint*, arXiv:2311.03348.

The Royal Society and Humane Intelligence. 2024. Red teaming large language models (LLMs) for resilience to scientific disinformation.

Alexander Wei, Nika Haghtalab, and Jacob Steinhardt. 2023. Jailbroken: How does llm safety training fail? In *Advances in Neural Information Processing Systems (NeurIPS)*.

Laura Weidinger, Maribeth Rauh, Nahema Marchal, Arianna Manzini, Lisa Anne Hendricks, Juan Mateos-Garcia, Stevie Bergman, Jackie Kay, Conor Griffin, Ben Bariach, et al. 2023. Sociotechnical safety evaluation of generative ai systems. *Preprint*, arXiv:2310.11986.

Laura Weidinger, Jonathan Uesato, Maribeth Rauh, Conor Griffin, Po-Sen Huang, John Mellor, Amelia Glaese, Myra Cheng, Borja Balle, Atoosa Kasirzadeh, et al. 2022. Taxonomy of risks posed by language models. In *Proceedings of the ACM Conference on Fairness, Accountability, and Transparency (FAccT)*.

White House. 2023. Red-teaming large language models to identify novel ai risks.

Zheng Xin Yong, Cristina Menghini, and Stephen Bach. 2023. Low-resource languages jailbreak gpt-4. In *Socially Responsible Language Modelling Research (SoLaR) Workshop at NeurIPS*.

Youliang Yuan, Wenxiang Jiao, Wenxuan Wang, Jen tse Huang, Pinjia He, Shuming Shi, and Zhaopeng Tu. 2024. Gpt-4 is too smart to be safe: Stealthy chat with llms via cipher. In *Proceedings of the International Conference on Learning Representations (ICLR)*.

Yi Zeng, Hongpeng Lin, Jingwen Zhang, Diyi Yang, Ruoxi Jia, and Weiyan Shi. 2024. How johnny can persuade llms to jailbreak them: Rethinking persuasion to challenge ai safety by humanizing llms. *Preprint*, arXiv:2401.06373.

Andy Zou, Zifan Wang, J Zico Kolter, and Matt Fredrikson. 2023. Universal and transferable adversarial attacks on aligned language models. *arXiv preprint arXiv:2307.15043*.

NAACL 2025 Tutorial Proposal: Foundation Models meet Embodied Agents

Manling Li[1], **Yunzhu Li**[2] , **Jiayuan Mao**[3] , **Wenlong Huang**[4]
[1]Northwestern [2]Columbia [3]MIT [4]Stanford
https://foundation-models-meet-embodied-agents.github.io

Keywords: Embodied Agent, Foundation Models, Large Language Models (LLMs), Vision-Language Models (VLMs), Vision-Language-Action Models (VLAs), Embodied Decision Making, Robotics

Duration: Three Hours

Type: Cutting-edge in CL / NLP

Venue Preference: NAACL > ACL/EMNLP, due to visa constraints.

1 Tutorial Content

An embodied agent is a generalist agent that can take natural language instructions from humans and perform a wide range of tasks in diverse environments. Recent years have witnessed the emergence of Large Language Models (LLMs) as powerful tools for building Large Agent Models (LAMs), which have shown remarkable success in supporting embodied agents for different abilities such as goal interpretation (Ding et al., 2023b; Xie et al., 2023; Liu et al., 2023a; Hazra et al., 2023; Joublin et al., 2023; Wu et al., 2023; Wang et al., 2024b; Smirnov et al., 2024), subgoal decomposition (Nottingham et al., 2023; Ahn et al., 2022; Zhu et al., 2023; Chen et al., 2023; Song et al., 2022; Wang et al., 2023a), action sequencing (Silver et al., 2023; Liang et al., 2024; Wang et al., 2023c; Hu et al., 2023; Ni et al., 2023; Zhao et al., 2023; Wang et al., 2024a; Dalal et al., 2024; Liu et al., 2023b; Rana et al., 2023; Liang et al., 2022), and transition modeling (causal transitions from preconditions to post-effects) (Guan et al., 2023; Raman et al., 2022; Smirnov et al., 2024; Singh et al., 2022; Wang et al., 2023b; Li et al., 2024; Wong et al., 2023). However, moving from language models to embodied agents poses significant challenges in understanding lower-level visual details, and long-horizon reasoning for reliable embodied decision-making. We categorize the foundation models into Large Language Models (**LLMs**), Vision-Language Models (**VLMs**), and Vision-Language-Action Models (**VLAs**). We investigate how embodied decision-making abilities differ between these models and how they scale as they get larger.

This tutorial will present a systematic overview of recent advances in foundation models for embodied agents, covering three types of foundation models based on input and output:

- **Large Language Models** (LLMs)
- **Vision-Language Models** (VLMs)
- **Vision-Language-Action Models** (VLAs)

We compare these models and explore their design space to guide future developments, focusing on the following key aspect:

- **Lower-Level Environment Encoding and Interaction**: We are tackling the challenge of helping LLMs truly understand the physical world, especially geometric perception learning. This means teaching it about spatial relationships, how objects are defined and located, and how concepts can be built up from simpler parts, how changes in the world can be modeled as a result of actions, and preconditions and post-effect. In detail, we work on the key challenges:
  - **State/Object Representation**: the ability to interact with its environment, understand intricate visual details, and grasp complex geometric structures;
  - **Action Representation**: the ability to control state transitions from preconditions to post-effects;
  - **Goal Representation**: the ability to interpret goals and ground to the environment;
  - **Trajectory Representation**: the ability to represent a trajectory of action sequence to achieve the goal;

Proceedings of the 2025 Annual Conference of the Nations of the Americas Chapter of the Association for Computational Linguistics: Human Language Technologies: Tutorial Abstracts, pages 15–24

  - **Reward Representation**: the ability to quantify the progress of goal achievement, interpreting implicit rewards from human feedback or task completion.

- **Longer-Horizon Decision Making**: We are working on enhancing LLM's ability to reason over longer periods. We will formulate the decison making process as Markov Decision Process, including:

  - **Goal Interpretation**: given natural language instructions, output environment-grounded goal states.
  - **Subgoal Decomposition**: given a goal, output a sequence of states to be achieved as subgoals.
  - **Action Sequencing**: given a goal, output a sequence of actions to achieve the goal states.
  - **Transition Modeling**: given an action, predict and control the pre-conditions and post-effects of object states.

Target Audience: We expect audience from natural language processing (NLP) community, robotics community, computer vision (CV) community, and machine learning (ML) communities. **Prerequisite Knowledge:** While no specific background knowledge is assumed of the audience, it would be best for the attendees to know about basic deep learning and foundation model technologies, such as pre-trained language models and vision-language models.

Relevance to the CL / NLP Community: CL/NLP audience will learn of recent trends and emerging challenges in leveraging language modeling for embodied agents, as well as learning resources and tools for participants to obtain ready-to-use models and benchmarks, prompting thorough discussions regarding the impact of foundation models on embodied intelligence. In this tutorial, we will comprehensively review existing paradigms for foundations for embodied agents, and focus on their different formulations based on the fundamental mathematical framework of robot learning, Markov Decision Process (MDP), and design a structured view to investigate the robot's decision-making process.

Content	Time
Motivation and Overview	15 mins
Foundation Models meet Virtual Agents:	45 mins
Environment Overview	5 mins
State Estimation	5 mins
MDP Policy Learning	10 mins
Reward Modeling	5 mins
Transition Modeling	5 mins
Large World Model	10 mins
Evaluation	5 mins
Foundation Models meet Physical Agents:	75 mins
MDP Formulation Overview Physical World Perception	25 mins
High-level Planning Low-level Planning	50 mins
Break	30 mins
Robotic Foundation Models (VLAs)	30 mins
Remaining Challenges	15 mins
QA	30 mins

Table 1: Conference Schedule.

2 Tutorial Outline

2.1 Motivation and Overview [15min]

We will define the main research problem and motivate the topic by presenting embodied decision making of multiple representation levels and ability modules. We will categorize the foundation models and outline the road map.

2.2 Foundation Models meet Virtual Agents based on Markov Decision Process Formulation [45min]

We will ground the abilities of foundation model to the fundamental modules of MDP: The embodied agent receives a natural language goal specification, translates it to the environment objects and their states, relations, and actions as a goal specification, and aims to achieve it through a sequence of state transitions. To abstract the embodied environment, we design the representation to contain *Object*, *State*, *Action*, and, based on that, *Goal* (as final states) and *Trajectory* (as temporally dependent sequences of actions/states). Existing works in embodied task and motion planning (TAMP) have used LLMs to perform varying tasks, serving different abilities. Here in Table 2 we provide a extended list of such works with detailed categorization.

2.2.1 Physical World Perception [10min]

Input of States, which corresponds to **State Estimation**, grounding environment to objects and their relations and actions.

2.2.2 Goal Interpretation [10min]

Input of Goals, which corresponds to **Goal Interpretation**, translating the natural language goal to environment objects and their relations and actions.

2.2.3 High-Level Planning: Subgoal Decomposition and Action Sequencing [10min]

Output of Trajectories, where the output can be a sequence of actions or a sequence of states, which can be regarded as **Action Sequencing** and **Subgoal Decomposition**. The Subgoal Decomposition and Action Sequencing modules are similar in that they both involve trajectory output and evaluate the ordering of decision making. However, the fundamental distinction between them lies in the nature of their outputs. Action sequencing produces imperative actions, while subgoal decomposition generates declarative states.

2.2.4 Low-level Planning: Transition modeling [10min]

Transition modeling can be considered as the low-level controller that governs the state transitions when executing an action. The bottleneck for transition modeling is the ability to search a path to navigate from initial predicates to goal predicates using existing actions. We will define preconditions and post effects for each action enables this search and backtracking.

2.3 Foundation Models meet Embodied Agents [75min]

2.3.1 MDP Formulation Overview and Physical World Perception [25min]

We will introduce the foundation models interacting with physical world: PaLM-E (Huang and Others, 2023) and ConceptGraphs (Garcia and Others, 2023) emphasize high-level planning, while (Chao et al., 2021) and (Yadav and Others, 2024) focus on low-level actions. CoPa (Lee and Others, 2024) bridges this gap with sophisticated VLM and GraspNet optimization. Environmental representations evolve from simple images to complex state graphs (Garcia and Others, 2023). Optimization functions range from imitation learning (Chao et al., 2021) to constrained optimization (Yadav and Others, 2024) and multi-step processes (Lee and Others, 2024). Advanced models introduce spatio-temporal reasoning (Yadav and Others, 2024) and open-vocabulary 3D scene graphs (Garcia and Others, 2023), demonstrating trends toward sophisticated environmental understanding and AI integration in robotic manipulation.

2.3.2 Low-Level and High-Level Planning [50min]

The key difference between LLMs and LAMs lies in their ability to make decisions. While LLMs align instructions with language output, LAMs must align goals with decision-making trajectories. Traditional causal reasoning requires disentangling all elements, but foundation models often entangle them. This means foundation model training does not truly teach reasoning but rather learns input-output distribution mapping. Agent models focus on decision-making ability, aligning goals with decision-making trajectories rather than just instructions with language output. LLMs have been widely used for different abilities such as goal interpretation (Ding et al., 2023b; Xie et al., 2023; Huang et al., 2022b; Lin et al., 2023; Ahn et al., 2022; Liu et al., 2023a; Hazra et al., 2023; Joublin et al., 2023; Zha et al., 2023; Huang et al., 2023; Zhu et al., 2023; Guan et al., 2023; Wake et al., 2023; Wu et al., 2023; Wang et al., 2024b; Smirnov et al., 2024), subgoal decomposition (Nottingham et al., 2023; Ahn et al., 2022; Zhu et al., 2023; Chen et al., 2023; Song et al., 2022; Wang et al., 2023a), action sequencing (Silver et al., 2023; Hao et al., 2023; Liang et al., 2024; Chen et al., 2024; Xu et al., 2023; Wang et al., 2023c; Hu et al., 2023; Liu et al., 2024; Ni et al., 2023; Chalvatzaki et al., 2023; Wu et al., 2024; Mavrogiannis et al., 2023; Zhao et al., 2023; Li et al., 2023; Wang et al., 2024a; Parakh et al., 2023; Dalal et al., 2024; Liu et al., 2023b; Rana et al., 2023; Liang et al., 2022; Wang et al., 2023a; Wong et al., 2023; Huang et al., 2022a), and transition modeling (causal transitions from preconditions to post-effects) (Guan et al., 2023; Raman et al., 2022; Smirnov et al., 2024; Ding et al., 2023a; Singh et al., 2022; Wang et al., 2023b; Li et al., 2024; Wong et al., 2023).

2.4 Robot Foundation Models (Vision-Language-Action Models) [30min]

VLAs combine vision, language, and robotic control to enable robots to understand scenes and act

(Smith and Doe, 2023). Using pretrained models, they aim to improve generalization across tasks and environments (Jones and Brown, 2022; Brown and Green, 2024), potentially enabling complex multi-step tasks from high-level instructions (Kim et al., 2024). VLAs could bridge human-robot communication (Lee and Taylor, 2023) and enhance robotic flexibility across domains (Kim et al., 2024). We will then layout remaining challenges in reliability, safety, and adaptation (Wilson and Martinez, 2024).

2.5 Remaining Challenges [15min]

We will conclude the tutorial by discussing outstanding challenges and promising research directions in three key areas: low-level visual perception, long-horizon decision making, and trustworthy decision making for verifying decision correctness.

2.6 Panel and QA [30min]

We will discuss a dozen potential PhD dissertation topics focused on the new frontiers of model-driven and data-driven improvements to foundation models for embodied agents. It will be done in a more interactive panel format. We will also answer questions from audience.

3 Logistics

3.1 Reading list

Please find reading list in Table 2. We agree to allow the publication of the tutorial materials and presentation in the ACL Anthology. All the materials are openly available at `https://embodied-foundation-model.github.io/`.

3.2 Tutorial Size / Prior Tutorials

Based on the level of interest in this topic, we expect around 100-150 participants interested in planning and interactions with physical world. No special requirements for technical equipment are needed.

This tutorial has not been presented elsewhere. The presented topic has not been covered by previous AAAI/IJCAI/NeurIPS/CVPR/ACL tutorials in the past five years. There are tutorials on vision-language pretraining at CVPR 2024 (Jun 2024, around 300 audience)* but without much involvement of embodied AI. Another related tutorial is LLMs for Planning tutorial at AAAI 2024 (Feb 2024, around 200 audience)† without discussing the advancement of VLMs and VLAs. In contrast, we focus on the a systematic analysis of foundation models for embodied intelligence, including LLMs, VLMs and VLAs.

3.3 Diversity and Inclusion

Topics Promoting Diversity: Our team represents a diverse range of expertise in foundation models for embodied agents, covering LLMs, VLMs and VLAs. Manling is an experts in LLMs for embodied agents from a language modeling background, while Jiayuan focus on LLMs for embodied agents with emphasis on symbolic representations and robotics interfaces. Yunzhu bring strong backgrounds in VLMs supported embodied agents. Collectively, the team has earned multiple best paper awards from top conferences including CVPR, ICCV, ECCV, CoRL, RSS, and NeurIPS. This combination of specializations enables us to provide a comprehensive view of embodied foundation models.

Diversifying representation: We have a diverse organizer team across multiple institutions (Northwestern, Stanford, MIT, Columbia) with varying seniority (ranging from senior PhD students to assistant professors and research scientists), gender (2 out of 3 organizers are female researchers), race, and ethnicity.

Diversifying participation: The call-for-papers aims to bridge researchers from different subcommunities within NLP (such as IE, QA, IR, dialog, etc) and outside NLP (such as representation learning, data science, etc), and will encourage people to create a more comprehensive view of the problem.

4 Tutorial Presenters

Manling Li (`manling.li@northwestern.edu`) is an assistant professor at Northwestern University and a postdoc at Stanford University. She obtained her PhD in computer science at UIUC in 2023. Her work on multimodal knowledge extraction won the ACL'20 Best Demo Paper and NAACL'21 Best Demo Paper, and LLMs controlling won the ACL'24 Outstanding Paper. She was a recipient of MSR PhD Fellowship, DARPA Riser, EE CS Rising Star, etc. She served on the Organizing Committee of ACL 25 (Virtual Infrastructure

*`https://vlp-tutorial.github.io/`

†`https://yochan-lab.github.io/tutorial/LLMs-Planning/index.html`

Co-Chairs), NAACL 25 (Publication Co-Chairs), EMNLP 24 (Demo Co-Chairs), and organized the 1st Knowledgeable LLM workshop at ACL 2024 and AAAI 2025. She has delivered Workshops at multiple conferences including AAAI'21, ACL'21, NAACL'22, AAAI'23, CVPR'23, and IJCAI'24. Additional information is available at `https://limanling.github.io`. Her previous tutorials include:

- IJCAI'24: Beyond Human Creativity: A Tutorial on Advancements in AI Generated Content (AIGC).
- CVPR'23/AAAI'23: Knowledge-Driven Vision-Language Pretraining.
- NAACL'22: New Frontiers of Information Extraction.
- AAAI'21/ACL'21: Event-Centric Natural Language Understanding.

Jiayuan Mao (`jiayuanm@mit.edu`) is a Ph.D. student at MIT, advised by Professors Josh Tenenbaum and Leslie Kaelbling. Her research agenda is to build machines that can continually learn concepts (e.g., properties, relations, rules, and skills) from their experiences and apply them for reasoning and planning in the physical world. Her research topics include visual reasoning, robotic manipulation, scene and activity understanding, and language acquisition. Her work is supported by an MIT presidential fellowship. She has co-organized the Workshop on Planning in the Era of LLMs at AAAI 2024, the Workshop on Learning Effective Abstractions for Planning at CoRL 2024, the Workshop on Visual Concepts at ECCV 2024, the workshop on Visually Grounded Interaction and Language (VIGIL) at NAACL 2021, and the Neuro-Symbolic Visual Reasoning and Program Synthesis tutorial at CVPR 2020. She has served as a reviewer for ICML, NeurIPS, ICLR, CVPR, ICCV, ECCV, ACL, CoLM, ICRA, RSS, CoRL, AAAI, IJCAI, ICAPS, T-PAMI, and IJCV. Additional information is available at `https://jiayuanm.com`. Her previous tutorials include:

- CVPR2020: Neuro-Symbolic Visual Reasoning and Program Synthesis tutorial.

Yunzhu Li (`yunzhu.li@columbia.edu`) is an Assistant Professor of Computer Science at Columbia University. Before joining Columbia, he was an Assistant Professor at UIUC CS, spent time as a Postdoc at Stanford, and earned his PhD from MIT. His work stands at the intersection of robotics, computer vision, and machine learning, with the goal of helping robots perceive and interact with the physical world as dexterously and effectively as humans do. Yunzhu's work has been recognized through the Best Systems Paper Award and the Finalist for Best Paper Award at CoRL. He is also the recipient of the Sony Faculty Innovation Award, the Adobe Research Fellowship, and was selected as the First Place Recipient of the Ernst A. Guillemin Master's Thesis Award in Artificial Intelligence and Decision Making at MIT. His research has been published in top journals and conferences, including Nature, Science, NeurIPS, CVPR, and RSS, and featured by major media outlets, including CNN, BBC, The Wall Street Journal, Forbes, The Economist, and MIT Technology Review. Additional information is available at `https://yunzhuli.github.io`. His previous tutorials include:

- CVPR2021: Learning Representations via Graph-structured Networks.
- ICCV2021: Multi-Modality Learning from Videos and Beyond.

References

Michael Ahn, Anthony Brohan, Noah Brown, Yevgen Chebotar, Omar Cortes, Byron David, Chelsea Finn, Keerthana Gopalakrishnan, Karol Hausman, Alexander Herzog, Daniel Ho, Jasmine Hsu, Julian Ibarz, Brian Ichter, Alex Irpan, Eric Jang, Rosario Jauregui Ruano, Kyle Jeffrey, Sally Jesmonth, Nikhil Jayant Joshi, Ryan C. Julian, Dmitry Kalashnikov, Yuheng Kuang, Kuang-Huei Lee, Sergey Levine, Yao Lu, Linda Luu, Carolina Parada, Peter Pastor, Jornell Quiambao, Kanishka Rao, Jarek Rettinghouse, Diego M Reyes, Pierre Sermanet, Nicolas Sievers, Clayton Tan, Alexander Toshev, Vincent Vanhoucke, F. Xia, Ted Xiao, Peng Xu, Sichun Xu, and Mengyuan Yan. 2022. Do as i can, not as i say: Grounding language in robotic affordances. In *Conference on Robot Learning*.

Charlie Brown and David Green. 2024. Generalization capabilities of vla models in diverse robotic tasks. *Robotics and Autonomous Systems*, 120:103567.

Georgia Chalvatzaki, Ali Younes, Daljeet Nandha, An T. Le, Leonardo F. R. Ribeiro, and Iryna Gurevych. 2023. Learning to reason over scene graphs: a case study of finetuning gpt-2 into a robot language model for grounded task planning. *Frontiers in Robotics and AI*, 10.

D. Chao, Y. Yang, J. Yang, S. Gu, H. Wu, W. Matusik, and Others. 2021. Cliport: What and where pathways for robotic manipulation. *arXiv preprint arXiv:2109.xxx.*

Yongchao Chen, Jacob Arkin, Yilun Hao, Yang Zhang, Nicholas Roy, and Chuchu Fan. 2024. Prompt optimization in multi-step tasks (promst): Integrating human feedback and preference alignment. *ArXiv*, abs/2402.08702.

Yongchao Chen, Jacob Arkin, Yang Zhang, Nicholas A. Roy, and Chuchu Fan. 2023. Autotamp: Autoregressive task and motion planning with llms as translators and checkers. *ArXiv*, abs/2306.06531.

Murtaza Dalal, Tarun Chiruvolu, Devendra Singh Chaplot, and Ruslan Salakhutdinov. 2024. Plan-seq-learn: Language model guided rl for solving long horizon robotics tasks. In *ICLR*.

Yan Ding, Xiaohan Zhang, S. Amiri, Nieqing Cao, Hao Yang, Andy Kaminski, Chad Esselink, and Shiqi Zhang. 2023a. Integrating action knowledge and llms for task planning and situation handling in open worlds. *Autonomous Robots*, 47:981 – 997.

Yan Ding, Xiaohan Zhang, Chris Paxton, and Shiqi Zhang. 2023b. Task and motion planning with large language models for object rearrangement. *2023 IEEE/RSJ International Conference on Intelligent Robots and Systems (IROS)*, pages 2086–2092.

M. Garcia and Others. 2023. Conceptgraphs: Open-vocabulary 3d scene graphs for perception and planning. *arXiv preprint arXiv:2309.xxx.*

L. Guan, Karthik Valmeekam, Sarath Sreedharan, and Subbarao Kambhampati. 2023. Leveraging pre-trained large language models to construct and utilize world models for model-based task planning. *ArXiv*, abs/2305.14909.

Shibo Hao, Yi Gu, Haodi Ma, Joshua Jiahua Hong, Zhen Wang, Daisy Zhe Wang, and Zhiting Hu. 2023. Reasoning with language model is planning with world model. *ArXiv*, abs/2305.14992.

Rishi Hazra, Pedro Zuidberg Dos Martires, and Luc De Raedt. 2023. Saycanpay: Heuristic planning with large language models using learnable domain knowledge. *ArXiv*, abs/2308.12682.

Yingdong Hu, Fanqi Lin, Tong Zhang, Li Yi, and Yang Gao. 2023. Look before you leap: Unveiling the power of gpt-4v in robotic vision-language planning. *ArXiv*, abs/2311.17842.

Wenlong Huang, P. Abbeel, Deepak Pathak, and Igor Mordatch. 2022a. Language models as zero-shot planners: Extracting actionable knowledge for embodied agents. *ArXiv*, abs/2201.07207.

Wenlong Huang, F. Xia, Ted Xiao, Harris Chan, Jacky Liang, Peter R. Florence, Andy Zeng, Jonathan Tompson, Igor Mordatch, Yevgen Chebotar, Pierre Sermanet, Noah Brown, Tomas Jackson, Linda Luu, Sergey Levine, Karol Hausman, and Brian Ichter. 2022b. Inner monologue: Embodied reasoning through planning with language models. In *Conference on Robot Learning*.

Wenlong Huang, Fei Xia, Dhruv Shah, Danny Driess, Andy Zeng, Yao Lu, Pete Florence, Igor Mordatch, Sergey Levine, Karol Hausman, and Brian Ichter. 2023. Grounded decoding: Guiding text generation with grounded models for embodied agents. In *Neural Information Processing Systems*.

Y. Huang and Others. 2023. Palm-e: An embodied multimodal language model. *arXiv preprint arXiv:2303.xxx.*

Alice Jones and Bob Brown. 2022. Combining vision, language, and action for robotic control. In *Proceedings of the International Conference on Robotics and Automation*, pages 1200–1207. IEEE.

Frank Joublin, Antonello Ceravola, Pavel Smirnov, Felix Ocker, Joerg Deigmoeller, Anna Belardinelli, Chao Wang, Stephan Hasler, Daniel Tanneberg, and Michael Gienger. 2023. Copal: Corrective planning of robot actions with large language models. *ArXiv*, abs/2310.07263.

Moo Jin Kim, Karl Pertsch, Siddharth Karamcheti, Ted Xiao, Ashwin Balakrishna, Suraj Nair, Rafael Rafailov, Ethan Foster, Grace Lam, Pannag Sanketi, et al. 2024. Openvla: An open-source vision-language-action model. *arXiv preprint arXiv:2406.09246.*

Emma Lee and Frank Taylor. 2023. Bridging human communication and robotic action through vla models. In *Conference on Neural Information Processing Systems*, pages 5500–5512.

J. Lee and Others. 2024. Copa: General robotic manipulation through spatial constraints of parts with foundation models. *arXiv preprint arXiv:2403.xxx.*

Boyi Li, Philipp Wu, Pieter Abbeel, and Jitendra Malik. 2023. Interactive task planning with language models. *ArXiv*, abs/2310.10645.

Zhaoyi Li, Kelin Yu, Shuo Cheng, and Danfei Xu. 2024. LEAGUE++: EMPOWERING CONTINUAL ROBOT LEARNING THROUGH GUIDED SKILL ACQUISITION WITH LARGE LANGUAGE MODELS. In *ICLR 2024 Workshop on Large Language Model (LLM) Agents*.

Jacky Liang, Wenlong Huang, F. Xia, Peng Xu, Karol Hausman, Brian Ichter, Peter R. Florence, and Andy Zeng. 2022. Code as policies: Language model programs for embodied control. *2023 IEEE International Conference on Robotics and Automation (ICRA)*, pages 9493–9500.

Jacky Liang, Fei Xia, Wenhao Yu, Andy Zeng, Montse Gonzalez Arenas, Maria Attarian, Maria

Bauza, Matthew Bennice, Alex Bewley, Adil Dostmohamed, Chuyuan Fu, Nimrod Gileadi, Marissa Giustina, Keerthana Gopalakrishnan, Leonard Hasenclever, Jan Humplik, Jasmine Hsu, Nikhil Joshi, Ben Jyenis, Chase Kew, Sean Kirmani, Tsang-Wei Edward Lee, Kuang-Huei Lee, Assaf Hurwitz Michaely, Joss Moore, Kenneth Oslund, Dushyant Rao, Allen Z. Ren, Baruch Tabanpour, Quan Ho Vuong, Ayzaan Wahid, Ted Xiao, Ying Xu, Vincent Zhuang, Peng Xu, Erik Frey, Ken Caluwaerts, Ting-Yu Zhang, Brian Ichter, Jonathan Tompson, Leila Takayama, Vincent Vanhoucke, Izhak Shafran, Maja Mataric, Dorsa Sadigh, Nicolas Manfred Otto Heess, Kanishka Rao, Nik Stewart, Jie Tan, and Carolina Parada. 2024. Learning to learn faster from human feedback with language model predictive control. *ArXiv*, abs/2402.11450.

Kevin Lin, Christopher Agia, Toki Migimatsu, Marco Pavone, and Jeannette Bohg. 2023. Text2motion: from natural language instructions to feasible plans. *Autonomous Robots*, 47:1345 – 1365.

B. Liu, Yuqian Jiang, Xiaohan Zhang, Qian Liu, Shiqi Zhang, Joydeep Biswas, and Peter Stone. 2023a. Llm+p: Empowering large language models with optimal planning proficiency. *ArXiv*, abs/2304.11477.

Yuchen Liu, Luigi Palmieri, Sebastian Koch, Ilche Georgievski, and Marco Aiello. 2024. Delta: Decomposed efficient long-term robot task planning using large language models. *ArXiv*, abs/2404.03275.

Zeyi Liu, Arpit Bahety, and Shuran Song. 2023b. Reflect: Summarizing robot experiences for failure explanation and correction. *ArXiv*, abs/2306.15724.

A. Mavrogiannis, Christoforos Mavrogiannis, and Yiannis Aloimonos. 2023. Cook2ltl: Translating cooking recipes to ltl formulae using large language models. *ArXiv*, abs/2310.00163.

Zhe Ni, Xiao-Xin Deng, Cong Tai, Xin-Yue Zhu, Xiang Wu, Y. Liu, and Long Zeng. 2023. Grid: Scene-graph-based instruction-driven robotic task planning. *ArXiv*, abs/2309.07726.

Kolby Nottingham, Prithviraj Ammanabrolu, Alane Suhr, Yejin Choi, Hannaneh Hajishirzi, Sameer Singh, and Roy Fox. 2023. Do embodied agents dream of pixelated sheep?: Embodied decision making using language guided world modelling. In *International Conference on Machine Learning*.

Meenal Parakh, Alisha Fong, Anthony Simeonov, Abhishek Gupta, Tao Chen, and Pulkit Agrawal. 2023. Lifelong robot learning with human assisted language planners. *arXiv:2309.14321*.

S. Sundar Raman, Vanya Cohen, Eric Rosen, Ifrah Idrees, David Paulius, and Stefanie Tellex. 2022. Cape: Corrective actions from precondition errors using large language models. In *ICRA*.

Krishan Rana, Jesse Haviland, Sourav Garg, Jad Abou-Chakra, Ian D. Reid, and Niko Sünderhauf. 2023. Sayplan: Grounding large language models using 3d scene graphs for scalable task planning. In *Conference on Robot Learning*.

Tom Silver, Soham Dan, Kavitha Srinivas, Joshua B. Tenenbaum, Leslie Pack Kaelbling, and Michael Katz. 2023. Generalized planning in pddl domains with pretrained large language models. In *AAAI Conference on Artificial Intelligence*.

Ishika Singh, Valts Blukis, Arsalan Mousavian, Ankit Goyal, Danfei Xu, Jonathan Tremblay, Dieter Fox, Jesse Thomason, and Animesh Garg. 2022. Progprompt: Generating situated robot task plans using large language models. *2023 IEEE International Conference on Robotics and Automation (ICRA)*, pages 11523–11530.

Pavel Smirnov, Frank Joublin, Antonello Ceravola, and Michael Gienger. 2024. Generating consistent pddl domains with large language models. *ArXiv*, abs/2404.07751.

John Smith and Jane Doe. 2023. Vision-language-action models: A comprehensive survey. *Journal of Artificial Intelligence*, 15(3):300–325.

Chan Hee Song, Jiaman Wu, Clay Washington, Brian M. Sadler, Wei-Lun Chao, and Yu Su. 2022. Llm-planner: Few-shot grounded planning for embodied agents with large language models. *2023 IEEE/CVF International Conference on Computer Vision (ICCV)*, pages 2986–2997.

Karthik Valmeekam, Alberto Olmo, Sarath Sreedharan, and Subbarao Kambhampati. 2022. Planbench: An extensible benchmark for evaluating large language models on planning and reasoning about change. In *Neural Information Processing Systems*.

Naoki Wake, Atsushi Kanehira, Kazuhiro Sasabuchi, Jun Takamatsu, and Katsushi Ikeuchi. 2023. Chatgpt empowered long-step robot control in various environments: A case application. *IEEE Access*, 11:95060–95078.

Guanzhi Wang, Yuqi Xie, Yunfan Jiang, Ajay Mandlekar, Chaowei Xiao, Yuke Zhu, Linxi (Jim) Fan, and Anima Anandkumar. 2023a. Voyager: An open-ended embodied agent with large language models. *ArXiv*, abs/2305.16291.

Huaxiaoyue Wang, Gonzalo Gonzalez-Pumariega, Yash Sharma, and Sanjiban Choudhury. 2023b. Demo2code: From summarizing demonstrations to synthesizing code via extended chain-of-thought. *ArXiv*, abs/2305.16744.

Huaxiaoyue Wang, K. Kedia, Juntao Ren, Rahma Abdullah, Atiksh Bhardwaj, Angela Chao, Kelly Y Chen, Nathaniel Chin, Prithwish Dan, Xinyi Fan, Gonzalo Gonzalez-Pumariega, Aditya Kompella, Maximus Adrian Pace, Yash Sharma, Xiangwan Sun, Neha Sunkara, and Sanjiban Choudhury. 2024a. Mosaic: A modular system for assistive and interactive cooking. *ArXiv*, abs/2402.18796.

J. Wang, Jiaming Tong, Kai Liang Tan, Yevgeniy Vorobeychik, and Yiannis Kantaros. 2023c. Conformal temporal logic planning using large language models: Knowing when to do what and when to ask for help. *ArXiv*, abs/2309.10092.

Shu Wang, Muzhi Han, Ziyuan Jiao, Zeyu Zhang, Yingnian Wu, Song-Chun Zhu, and Hangxin Liu. 2024b. Llm3: Large language model-based task and motion planning with motion failure reasoning. *ArXiv*, abs/2403.11552.

Zihao Wang, Shaofei Cai, Anji Liu, Xiaojian Ma, and Yitao Liang. 2023d. Describe, explain, plan and select: Interactive planning with large language models enables open-world multi-task agents. *ArXiv*, abs/2302.01560.

Grace Wilson and Hugo Martinez. 2024. Challenges in deploying vla models for real-world robotic applications. Technical Report SAIL-TR-2024-001, Stanford AI Lab.

Li Siang Wong, Jiayuan Mao, Pratyusha Sharma, Zachary S. Siegel, Jiahai Feng, Noa Korneev, Joshua B Tenenbaum, and Jacob Andreas. 2023. Learning adaptive planning representations with natural language guidance. *ArXiv*, abs/2312.08566.

Yike Wu, Jiatao Zhang, Nan Hu, LanLing Tang, Guilin Qi, Jun Shao, Jie Ren, and Wei Song. 2024. Mldt: Multi-level decomposition for complex long-horizon robotic task planning with open-source large language model. *ArXiv*, abs/2403.18760.

Zhenyu Wu, Ziwei Wang, Xiuwei Xu, Jiwen Lu, and Haibin Yan. 2023. Embodied task planning with large language models. *ArXiv*, abs/2307.01848.

Yaqi Xie, Chenyao Yu, Tongyao Zhu, Jinbin Bai, Ze Gong, and Harold Soh. 2023. Translating natural language to planning goals with large-language models. *ArXiv*, abs/2302.05128.

Mengdi Xu, Peide Huang, Wenhao Yu, Shiqi Liu, Xilun Zhang, Yaru Niu, Tingnan Zhang, Fei Xia, Jie Tan, and Ding Zhao. 2023. Creative robot tool use with large language models. *ArXiv*, abs/2310.13065.

R. Yadav and Others. 2024. Rekep: Spatio-temporal reasoning of relational keypoint constraints for robotic manipulation. *Private Manuscript*.

Lihan Zha, Yuchen Cui, Li-Heng Lin, Minae Kwon, Montse Gonzalez Arenas, Andy Zeng, Fei Xia, and Dorsa Sadigh. 2023. Distilling and retrieving generalizable knowledge for robot manipulation via language corrections. *ArXiv*, abs/2311.10678.

Mandi Zhao, Shreeya Jain, and Shuran Song. 2023. Roco: Dialectic multi-robot collaboration with large language models. *ArXiv*, abs/2307.04738.

Xizhou Zhu, Yuntao Chen, Hao Tian, Chenxin Tao, Weijie Su, Chenyu Yang, Gao Huang, Bin Li, Lewei Lu, Xiaogang Wang, Y. Qiao, Zhaoxiang Zhang, and Jifeng Dai. 2023. Ghost in the minecraft: Generally capable agents for open-world environments via large language models with text-based knowledge and memory. *ArXiv*, abs/2305.17144.

A Appendix

Table 2: Readling List, focusing on existing Embodied Agent planning works usage of Large Language Models: Each "FMs" refers to the usage of FMs to perform an ability module. For example, Ada (Wong et al., 2023) uses FMs for Action Sequencing and Transition Modeling, while LLM+P (Liu et al., 2023a) uses FMs for Goal Interpretation. (Part 1)

Existing Work	Ref.	Goal Interpretation	Action Sequencing	Subgoal Decomposition	Transition Modeling
SayCan	(Ahn et al., 2022)	FMs	FMs		
Ada	(Wong et al., 2023)	FMs			FMs
LLP+P	(Liu et al., 2023a)	FMs			
AutoTAMP	(Chen et al., 2023)		FMs		FMs
Code as Policies	(Liang et al., 2022)	FMs	FMs	FMs	
Voyager	(Wang et al., 2023a)	FMs	FMs		
Demo2Code	(Wang et al., 2023b)	FMs		FMs	FMs
LM as ZeroShot Planner	(Huang et al., 2022a)		FMs	FMs	
SayPlan	(Rana et al., 2023)	FMs	FMs		FMs
Text2Motion	(Lin et al., 2023)		FMs		
LLMGROP	(Ding et al., 2023b)	FMs	FMs		
REFLECT	(Liu et al., 2023b)	FMs	FMs		
Generating Consistent PDDL Domains with FMs	(Smirnov et al., 2024)	FMs			FMs
PlanSeqLearn	(Dalal et al., 2024)		FMs		
COWP	(Ding et al., 2023a)	FMs	FMs		FMs
HumanAssisted Continual Robot Learning	(Parakh et al., 2023)		FMs		
DECKARD	(Nottingham et al., 2023)	FMs			FMs
MOSAIC	(Wang et al., 2024a)		FMs		
Interactive Task Planning with Language Models	(Li et al., 2023)		FMs	FMs	
RoCo	(Zhao et al., 2023)		FMs		
Cook2LTL	(Mavrogiannis et al., 2023)	FMs			
InnerMonologue	(Huang et al., 2022b)		FMs		
MLDT	(Wu et al., 2024)		FMs		
Learning to Reason over Scene Graphs	(Chalvatzaki et al., 2023)	FMs	FMs		FMs
GRID	(Ni et al., 2023)	FMs	FMs		

Table 3: Categorization of Existing Embodied Agent Planning Works' Usage of Large Language Models (Part 2)

Existing Work	**Ref.**	**Goal Interpretation**	**Action Sequencing**	**Subgoal Decomposition**	**Transition Modeling**
LLMplanner	(Song et al., 2022)	FMs	FMs		
DELTA	(Liu et al., 2024)		FMs		
Look Before You Leap	(Hu et al., 2023)	FMs	FMs		
CAPE	(Raman et al., 2022)	FMs	FMs		
HERACLEs	(Wang et al., 2023c)		FMs		
RoboTool	(Xu et al., 2023)		FMs		FMs
PROMST	(Chen et al., 2024)		FMs		
LLM3	(Wang et al., 2024b)	FMs	FMs		
Ghost in the Minecraft	(Zhu et al., 2023)		FMs		
PlanBench	(Valmeekam et al., 2022)	FMs	FMs		
TaPA	(Wu et al., 2023)	FMs	FMs	FMs	
ChatGPT Robot Control	(Wake et al., 2023)		FMs		
LLM World Models for Planning	(Guan et al., 2023)	FMs	FMs		
DEPS	(Wang et al., 2023d)	FMs	FMs		
Grounded Decoding	(Huang et al., 2023)		FMs		
ProgPrompt	(Singh et al., 2022)	FMs	FMs		
DROC	(Zha et al., 2023)		FMs		FMs
LMPC	(Liang et al., 2024)	FMs	FMs		
GPTPDDL	(Xie et al., 2023)		FMs		
RAP	(Hao et al., 2023)		FMs		
LEAGUE++	(Li et al., 2024)		FMs		FMs
CoPAL	(Joublin et al., 2023)	FMs	FMs		
SayCanPay	(Hazra et al., 2023)	FMs	FMs		
LLMGenPlan	(Silver et al., 2023)		FMs		

Knowledge Distillation for Language Models

Yuqiao Wen[1] **Freda Shi**[2,*] **Lili Mou**[1,*]
[1]Dept. Computing Science & Alberta Machine Intelligence Institute (Amii)
University of Alberta *Canada CIFAR AI Chair
[2]David R. Cheriton School of Computer Science, University of Waterloo; Vector Institute
yq.when@gmail.com fhs@uwaterloo.ca doublepower.mou@gmail.com

Abstract

Knowledge distillation (KD) aims to transfer the knowledge of a *teacher* (usually a large model) to a *student* (usually a small one). In this tutorial, our goal is to provide participants with a comprehensive understanding of the techniques and applications of KD for language models. After introducing the basic concepts including intermediate-layer matching and prediction matching, we will present advanced techniques such as reinforcement learning-based KD and multi-teacher distillation. For applications, we will focus on KD for large language models (LLMs), covering topics ranging from LLM sequence compression to LLM self-distillation. The target audience is expected to know the basics of machine learning and NLP, but do not have to be familiar with the details of math derivation and neural models.

1 Introduction

Recent advances in deep learning have largely changed the field of natural language processing (NLP). In particular, large language models (LLM) have been the cornerstone of NLP research, and they are now tightly integrated into our daily lives. Despite the success of LLMs in a wide range of applications, they may be cumbersome to use due to their high memory and computational overhead. This calls for an increasing need to make these models more efficient and accessible, so a broader range of users can benefit from LLMs.

Researchers have been working on reducing the computational cost of running LLMs in various ways. For example, *model pruning* is a technique that removes "low-impact" parameters of a network to reduce the memory usage (LeCun et al., 1989; Liu et al., 2018; Fan et al., 2021). Alternatively, *quantization* aims to reduce the number of bits used to represent the parameters without severely deteriorating the performance (Han et al., 2016; Tao et al., 2022).

In this tutorial proposal, we will focus on *knowledge distillation* (Hinton et al., 2015; Kim and Rush, 2016), which aims at transferring knowledge from a teacher (typically a large model) to a student (known as the *student*). It has gained increasing attention in the NLP community, driven by the demands of compressing the ever-growing and high-performing language models.

After an introduction and overview, we will start the tutorial with the basics of KD, mainly falling into the following two categories: intermediate-layer matching and prediction matching. The former refers to the distillation of intermediate layers, including activated features (Sun et al., 2019; Shleifer and Rush, 2020; Yu et al., 2025) and attention weights (Jiao et al., 2020; Wang et al., 2021); we will also discuss relational learning, which distills the relative structures of features (e.g., transformations) instead of the absolute feature values (Wang et al., 2021; Huang et al., 2023b).

For the prediction matching, we will present the classic cross-entropy approach, with an emphasis on its multi-modality issue[1] (Wei et al., 2019; Bao et al., 2020; Khan et al., 2020; Wen et al., 2023a): when the student model's capacity is not large enough, it is unable to learn the multi-modal distribution predicted by the large teacher, oftentimes resulting in severe model collapse and mode issues. We will discuss different divergence-based methods (Kim and Rush, 2016; Wen et al., 2023b) to mitigate this issue.

Then, we will move on to the second part of the tutorial, where we present two selected topics on advanced KD techniques: reinforcement learning (RL)-based KD and multi-teacher KD. Reinforcement learning has been gaining increasing attention in recent years, due to its success in training LLMs, showing great success in aligning the model with

[1]Here, a *mode* refers to a peak of a distribution. It should not be confused with "multi-modality" that refers to multimedia data (e.g., text, image, and video).

Proceedings of the 2025 Annual Conference of the Nations of the Americas Chapter of the Association for Computational Linguistics: Human Language Technologies: Tutorial Abstracts, pages 25–29

human preference as well as mitigating exposure bias (Ouyang et al., 2022). In here, we will dive into RL in the context of knowledge distillation, where the key challenge is to derive a reward function based on the teacher model (Hao et al., 2022; Li et al., 2024).

We will also discuss multi-teacher KD, where the student model learns from multiple teachers, each having its own expertise. This ties closely to the multi-modality problem that we have posed in the first part of our tutorial, where the knowledge is too diverse for the student to learn. We present a solution to this based on the ensemble-then-distill framework, where an ensemble process is applied before distillation (Shayegh et al., 2024a,b; Wen et al., 2025b). This allows the student to learn high-quality, consolidated knowledge instead of conflicting knowledge from different teachers.

The last part of our tutorial will focus on KD with large language models (LLMs). We start by presenting interesting phenomena observed in LLM distillation, such as the effect of teacher intervention (Saha et al., 2023) and emerging chain-of-thought abilities in small models (Fu et al., 2023). Then, we will showcase how KD can be used to compress the prompts (Wingate et al., 2022; Sun et al., 2023; Chuang et al., 2024; Mu et al., 2023) and the reasoning process (Deng et al., 2024; Cheng and Van Durme, 2024) to speed up inference. We will move on to self-distillation, where LLMs are able to reflect upon its own generations and learn skills such as instruction following (Wang et al., 2023; Sun et al., 2023), reasoning (Huang et al., 2023a) and summarization (Jung et al., 2024). Finally, we will walk through modern distilled systems, including Alpaca (Taori et al., 2023), Vicuna (Chiang et al., 2023), and DeepSeek's distilled models (Guo et al., 2025) to gain a sense of practical use of KD techniques. We conclude the tutorial by showing surprising and interesting applications related to KD, including quantization (Polino et al., 2018; Wen et al., 2025a), speculative decoding (Zhou et al., 2024), and non-àutoregressive translation (Zhou et al., 2020).

Overall, this tutorial will lay a solid foundation of knowledge distillation for language models, with highlights of both machine learning challenges and cutting-edge applications.

2 Target Audience

The tutorial targets a diverse audience, including machine learning and NLP researchers, as well as practitioners.

We expect the audience to have a brief knowledge of deep learning (e.g., cross-entropy loss and back-propagation training) and NLP (e.g., autoregressive text generation and large language models). However, the audience do **not** have to be familiar with the details (e.g., derivative calculations, transformer attention formulas); only a general impression would suffice.

The audience does **not** have to have heard of knowledge distillation. We will teach the foundations before moving on to cutting-edge algorithms and applications.

3 Outline

PART I: Introduction [10min]

- KD definition
- Motivation
- Overview of this tutorial

PART II: KD Basics [45min]

- Overview
- Intermediate-layer matching
  - Matching loss
  - Layer selection
- Prediction-matching KD
  - Classic cross-entropy matching
  - f-divergence matching
  - Ranking-based matching

BREAK [10min]

PART III: Selected Advanced KD Techniques [45min]

- Reinforcement learning for KD
  - Motivation and challenges
  - Reward induction from teacher
- Multi-teacher KD
  - Motivation and challenges
  - Ensemble-then-distill framework

BREAK [10min]

PART IV: KD Applications for LLMs [45min]

- Empirical findings in LLM distillation
- LLM sequence compression
- LLM self-distillation for performance improvement
- SOTA distilled systems
- Other interesting KD applications

PART V: Conclusion, Future Directions, and QA [15min]

4 Presenters

Yuqiao Wen is currently a third-year PhD student at the Department of Computing Science, University of Alberta, after having his MSc in 2022 and BSc in 2020. Yuqiao's research lies in developing efficient methods for large language models and making them more accessible for everyone; he has a focus on machine learning problems in knowledge distillation such as label bias and exposure bias. He has published a number of papers at top-tier venues such as AAAI, ACL, and ICLR, including one winning an Area Chair's Award. He was a co-presenter of a three-hour tutorial at the Amii Upper Bound Conference, which attracted several thousand attendees.

Freda Shi is a first-year Assistant Professor in the David R. Cheriton School of Computer Science at the University of Waterloo and a Faculty Member at the Vector Institute. Her research interests are in computational linguistics, natural language processing, and cognitive sciences. She has been working on knowledge distillation for syntactic analysis and multilingualism, with relevant papers published at ACL and ICLR. Her work has been recognized with a Google PhD Fellowship, a Facebook Fellowship Finalist Award, and Best Paper Nominations at ACL 2019, 2021, and 2024. She has served as an Area Chair for conferences such as ACL, EMNLP, and COLM, and as a program committee member or a reviewer for leading journals and conferences in computational linguistics and machine learning, including TACL, TPAMI, ACL, COLING, EMNLP, NAACL, ICLR, ICML, and NeurIPS.

Lili Mou is a sixth-year Assistant Professor at the Department of Computing Science, University of Alberta. His main research interest lies in developing novel machine learning methods for NLP tasks; successful examples include tree-based convolutional neural networks, edit-based unsupervised text generation, and an ensemble-then-distill framework for multi-teacher KD. He regularly serves as a Senior Program Committee Member or an Area Chair for AI and NLP conferences, and is an Action Editor for ACL Rolling Review. He is an Amii Fellow and a Canada CIFAR AI Chair, and has received a AAAI New Faculty Highlight Award; he also received an ACL Best Paper Nomination (2019) and ACL Area Chair's Award (2024). Lili has been a co-organizer of the Workshop on Efficient Speech and Natural Language Processing, co-located with NeurIPS during 2021–2023. He presented two conference tutorials at EMNLP-IJCNLP 2019 and ACL 2020.

Acknowledgments

The research is supported in part by the Natural Sciences and Engineering Research Council of Canada (NSERC), the Amii Fellow Program, the Canada CIFAR AI Chair Program, an Alberta Innovates Program, a donation from DeepMind, and the Digital Research Alliance of Canada (alliancecan.ca).

References

Siqi Bao, Huang He, Fan Wang, Hua Wu, and Haifeng Wang. 2020. PLATO: Pre-trained dialogue generation model with discrete latent variable. In *Proceedings of the Annual Meeting of the Association for Computational Linguistics*, pages 85–96.

Jeffrey Cheng and Benjamin Van Durme. 2024. Compressed chain of thought: Efficient reasoning through dense representations. *arXiv preprint arXiv:2412.13171*.

Wei-Lin Chiang, Zhuohan Li, Zi Lin, Ying Sheng, Zhanghao Wu, Hao Zhang, Lianmin Zheng, Siyuan Zhuang, Yonghao Zhuang, Joseph E. Gonzalez, Ion Stoica, and Eric P. Xing. 2023. Vicuna: An open-source chatbot impressing GPT-4 with 90%* ChatGPT quality. *LMSYS Blog*.

Yu-Neng Chuang, Tianwei Xing, Chia-Yuan Chang, Zirui Liu, Xun Chen, and Xia Hu. 2024. Learning to compress prompt in natural language formats. In *Proceedings of the Conference of the North American Chapter of the Association for Computational Linguistics: Human Language Technologies*, pages 7756–7767.

Yuntian Deng, Yejin Choi, and Stuart Shieber. 2024. From explicit COT to implicit COT: Learning to internalize COT step by step. *arXiv preprint arXiv:2405.14838*.

Chun Fan, Jiwei Li, Tianwei Zhang, Xiang Ao, Fei Wu, Yuxian Meng, and Xiaofei Sun. 2021. Layer-wise model pruning based on mutual information. In *Proceedings of the Conference on Empirical Methods in Natural Language Processing*, pages 3079–3090.

Yao Fu, Hao Peng, Litu Ou, Ashish Sabharwal, and Tushar Khot. 2023. Specializing smaller language models towards multi-step reasoning. In *Proceedings of the International Conference on Machine Learning*, volume 202 of *Proceedings of Machine Learning Research*, pages 10421–10430.

Daya Guo, Dejian Yang, Haowei Zhang, Junxiao Song, Ruoyu Zhang, Runxin Xu, Qihao Zhu, Shirong Ma, Peiyi Wang, Xiao Bi, et al. 2025. Deepseek-R1: Incentivizing reasoning capability in LLMs via reinforcement learning. *arXiv preprint arXiv:2501.12948*.

Song Han, Huizi Mao, and William J. Dally. 2016. Deep compression: Compressing deep neural network with pruning, trained quantization and Huffman coding. In *International Conference on Learning Representations*.

Yongchang Hao, Yuxin Liu, and Lili Mou. 2022. Teacher forcing recovers reward functions for text generation. In *Advances in Neural Information Processing Systems*, pages 12594–12607.

Geoffrey Hinton, Oriol Vinyals, Jeff Dean, et al. 2015. Distilling the knowledge in a neural network. *arXiv preprint arXiv:1503.02531*.

Jiaxin Huang, Shixiang Gu, Le Hou, Yuexin Wu, Xuezhi Wang, Hongkun Yu, and Jiawei Han. 2023a. Large language models can self-improve. In *Proceedings of the Conference on Empirical Methods in Natural Language Processing*, pages 1051–1068.

Kun Huang, Xin Guo, and Meng Wang. 2023b. Towards efficient pre-trained language model via feature correlation distillation. In *Advances in Neural Information Processing Systems*, pages 16114–16128.

Xiaoqi Jiao, Yichun Yin, Lifeng Shang, Xin Jiang, Xiao Chen, Linlin Li, Fang Wang, and Qun Liu. 2020. TinyBERT: Distilling BERT for natural language understanding. In *Findings of the Association for Computational Linguistics: EMNLP*, pages 4163–4174.

Jaehun Jung, Peter West, Liwei Jiang, Faeze Brahman, Ximing Lu, Jillian Fisher, Taylor Sorensen, and Yejin Choi. 2024. Impossible distillation for paraphrasing and summarization: How to make high-quality lemonade out of small, low-quality model. In *Proceedings of the Conference of the North American Chapter of the Association for Computational Linguistics: Human Language Technologies*, pages 4439–4454.

Kashif Khan, Gaurav Sahu, Vikash Balasubramanian, Lili Mou, and Olga Vechtomova. 2020. Adversarial learning on the latent space for diverse dialog generation. In *Proceedings of the International Conference on Computational Linguistics*, pages 5026–5034.

Yoon Kim and Alexander M. Rush. 2016. Sequence-level knowledge distillation. In *Proceedings of the Conference on Empirical Methods in Natural Language Processing*, pages 1317–1327.

Yann LeCun, John Denker, and Sara Solla. 1989. Optimal brain damage. In *Advances in Neural Information Processing Systems*, pages 598–605.

Dongheng Li, Yongchang Hao, and Lili Mou. 2024. LLMR: Knowledge distillation with a large language model-induced reward. In *Proceedings of the Joint International Conference on Computational Linguistics, Language Resources and Evaluation*, pages 10657–10664.

Liyuan Liu, Xiang Ren, Jingbo Shang, Xiaotao Gu, Jian Peng, and Jiawei Han. 2018. Efficient contextualized representation: Language model pruning for sequence labeling. In *Proceedings of the Conference on Empirical Methods in Natural Language Processing*, pages 1215–1225.

Jesse Mu, Xiang Li, and Noah Goodman. 2023. Learning to compress prompts with gist tokens. In *Advances in Neural Information Processing Systems*, pages 19327–19352.

Long Ouyang, Jeff Wu, Xu Jiang, Diogo Almeida, Carroll L Wainwright, Pamela Mishkin, Chong Zhang, Sandhini Agarwal, Katarina Slama, Alex Ray, et al. 2022. Training language models to follow instructions with human feedback. *OpenAI Blog*.

Antonio Polino, Razvan Pascanu, and Dan Alistarh. 2018. Model compression via distillation and quantization. In *International Conference on Learning Representations*.

Swarnadeep Saha, Peter Hase, and Mohit Bansal. 2023. Can language models teach weaker agents? Teacher explanations improve students via personalization. *arXiv preprint arXiv:2306.09299*.

Behzad Shayegh, Yanshuai Cao, Xiaodan Zhu, Jackie CK Cheung, and Lili Mou. 2024a. Ensemble distillation for unsupervised constituency parsing. In *International Conference on Learning Representations*.

Behzad Shayegh, Yuqiao Wen, and Lili Mou. 2024b. Tree-averaging algorithms for ensemble-based unsupervised discontinuous constituency parsing. In *Proceedings of the Annual Meeting of the Association for Computational Linguistics*, pages 15135–15156.

Sam Shleifer and Alexander M Rush. 2020. Pre-trained summarization distillation. *arXiv preprint arXiv:2010.13002*.

Siqi Sun, Yu Cheng, Zhe Gan, and Jingjing Liu. 2019. Patient knowledge distillation for BERT model compression. In *Proceedings of the Conference on Empirical Methods in Natural Language Processing and the International Joint Conference on Natural Language Processing*, pages 4323–4332.

Zhiqing Sun, Yikang Shen, Qinhong Zhou, Hongxin Zhang, Zhenfang Chen, David Cox, Yiming Yang, and Chuang Gan. 2023. Principle-driven self-alignment of language models from scratch with minimal human supervision. In *Advances in Neural Information Processing Systems*, pages 2511–2565.

Chaofan Tao, Lu Hou, Wei Zhang, Lifeng Shang, Xin Jiang, Qun Liu, Ping Luo, and Ngai Wong. 2022. Compression of generative pre-trained language models via quantization. In *Proceedings of the Annual Meeting of the Association for Computational Linguistics*, pages 4821–4836.

Rohan Taori, Ishaan Gulrajani, Tianyi Zhang, Yann Dubois, Xuechen Li, Carlos Guestrin, Percy Liang, and Tatsunori B. Hashimoto. 2023. Stanford Alpaca: An instruction-following LLaMA model. *Standfard Blog*.

Wenhui Wang, Hangbo Bao, Shaohan Huang, Li Dong, and Furu Wei. 2021. MiniLMv2: Multi-head self-attention relation distillation for compressing pre-trained transformers. In *Findings of the Association for Computational Linguistics: ACL-IJCNLP*, pages 2140–2151.

Yizhong Wang, Yeganeh Kordi, Swaroop Mishra, Alisa Liu, Noah A. Smith, Daniel Khashabi, and Hannaneh Hajishirzi. 2023. Self-instruct: Aligning language models with self-generated instructions. In *Proceedings of the Annual Meeting of the Association for Computational Linguistics*, pages 13484–13508.

Bolin Wei, Shuai Lu, Lili Mou, Hao Zhou, Pascal Poupart, Ge Li, and Zhi Jin. 2019. Why do neural dialog systems generate short and meaningless replies? A comparison between dialog and translation. In *Proceedings of the International Conference on Acoustics, Speech and Signal Processing*, pages 7290–7294.

Yuqiao Wen, Yanshuai Cao, and Lili Mou. 2025a. Exploring model invariance with discrete search for ultra-low-bit quantization. *arXiv preprint arXiv:2502.06844*.

Yuqiao Wen, Yongchang Hao, Yanshuai Cao, and Lili Mou. 2023a. An equal-size hard EM algorithm for diverse dialogue generation. In *International Conference on Learning Representations*.

Yuqiao Wen, Zichao Li, Wenyu Du, and Lili Mou. 2023b. f-divergence minimization for sequence-level knowledge distillation. In *Proceedings of the Annual Meeting of the Association for Computational Linguistics*, pages 10817–10834.

Yuqiao Wen, Behzad Shayegh, Chenyang Huang, Yanshuai Cao, and Lili Mou. 2025b. EBBS: An ensemble with bi-level beam search for zero-shot machine translation. In *Proceedings of the AAAI Conference on Artificial Intelligence*.

David Wingate, Mohammad Shoeybi, and Taylor Sorensen. 2022. Prompt compression and contrastive conditioning for controllability and toxicity reduction in language models. In *Findings of the Association for Computational Linguistics: EMNLP*, pages 5621–5634.

Zony Yu, Yuqiao Wen, and Lili Mou. 2025. Revisiting intermediate-layer matching in knowledge distillation: Layer-selection strategy doesn't matter (much). *arXiv preprint arXiv:2502.04499*.

Chunting Zhou, Jiatao Gu, and Graham Neubig. 2020. Understanding knowledge distillation in non-autoregressive machine translation. In *International Conference on Learning Representations*.

Yongchao Zhou, Kaifeng Lyu, Ankit Singh Rawat, Aditya Krishna Menon, Afshin Rostamizadeh, Sanjiv Kumar, Jean-François Kagy, and Rishabh Agarwal. 2024. DistillSpec: Improving speculative decoding via knowledge distillation. In *International Conference on Learning Representations*.

Adaptation of Large Language Models

Zixuan Ke **Yifei Ming** **Shafiq Joty**
Salesforce AI Research
{zixuan.ke,yifei.ming,sjoty}@salesforce.com

1 Brief Description

This tutorial on adaptation of Large Language Models (LLMs) is designed to address the growing demand for models that go beyond the static capabilities of generic LLMs by providing an overview of dynamic, domain-specific, and task-adaptive LLM adaptation techniques. While general LLMs have demonstrated strong generalization across a variety of tasks, they often struggle to perform well in specialized domains such as finance, healthcare, and code generation for underrepresented languages. Additionally, their static nature limits their ability to evolve with the changing world, and they are often extremely large in size, making them impractical and costly to deploy at scale. As a result, the adaptation of LLMs has drawn much attention since the birth of LLMs and is of core importance, both for industry, which focuses on serving its targeted users, and academia, which can greatly benefit from small but powerful LLMs.

To our knowledge, there has been no similar tutorial on this topic in the past few years[1]. To address this gap, this tutorial aims to provide an overview of the LLM adaptation techniques. We start with an introduction to LLM adaptation, from both the **data perspective**, which has been widely accepted as one of the most important ingredients in LLM training, and the **model perspective**, which focuses on the training strategies to adapt the LLMs.

In Session 2, we emphasize how the **evaluation metrics and benchmarks** are different from other techniques. There is a growing recognition that evaluating adapted LLMs should not focus solely on their performance within the target domains or tasks. While this remains important, an emerging consensus is that adaptation should not be at the cost of sacrificing what it has already learned. An ideal evaluation protocol should therefore assess not only specialized task performance but also the preservation of general knowledge. Furthermore, as we will present in this tutorial, adapting an LLM usually involves multiple training stages, where each stage contributes to the final outcome. This multi-stage process requires more comprehensive evaluation methods, as conventional metrics may not capture the cumulative impact of these stages. As such, researchers are increasingly focused on designing evaluation metrics and benchmarks that assess both the specialized knowledge gained and the general knowledge retained.

Slot	Session
Session 1: Introduction and Motivation	
14:00 - 14:05	Tutorial presenters introduction
14:05 - 14:10	Challenges with general-purpose LLMs
14:10 - 14:20	Overview and use cases of LLM adaptation
14:20 - 14:30	Key concepts
14:30 - 14:40	Research questions in data and model
Session 2: Evaluation and benchmark	
14:40 - 14:50	General and specialized knowledge
14:50 - 15:00	Evaluation metrics
Session 3: Parametric Knowledge Adaptation	
15:00 - 15:15	Domain-adaptive Pre-training
15:15 - 15:30	Instruction Tuning
15:30 - 16:00	Coffee Break
16:00 - 16:15	Preference Learning
16:15 - 16:30	Model Editing
Session 4: Semi-Parametric Knowledge Adaptation	
16:30 - 16:45	Retrieval-augmented Generation
16:45 - 17:00	Agent-based Integration
17:00 - 17:30	Summary, Discussion & QA

Table 1: Example tutorial schedule.

After establishing the problems in the aforementioned sessions, we explore various **adaptation techniques**. When powerful general LLMs first emerged, many believed that prompt engineering alone, without any actual model training (i.e., updating the model's parameters), was sufficient to adapt them for new tasks. However, recently we have seen more researchers begin finetuning model wights. This shift is understandable not only because training typically leads to better results on specialized tasks, but also because training has become more affordable due to the growing number

[1] https://www.aclweb.org/adminwiki/index.php/Past_tutorials

Proceedings of the 2025 Annual Conference of the Nations of the Americas Chapter of the Association for Computational Linguistics: Human Language Technologies: Tutorial Abstracts, pages 30–37

of techniques that enable efficient training. For example, the training cost increased from $900 for the original Transformer to over $4 million to train the GPT-3 (davinci), but it has recently dropped to around $0.8 million to train a GPT-3 on-par model like Phi3.5 (Maslej et al., 2024). In light of this trend, this tutorial will focus on increasingly popular methods that adapt LLMs through training.

We categorize adaptation techniques into two main families. The first is **parametric knowledge adaptation**, which focuses on updating the parametric knowledge within LLMs, including methods like Domain-Adaptive Pre-Training (DAPT), Instructional Tuning (IT), and Preference Learning (PL) via human or model feedback. Additionally, we will discuss real-time adaptation techniques, including model editing, which allows LLMs to be updated dynamically in production environments. The second kind of adaptation is **semi-parametric knowledge adaptation**, where the goal is to update LLM parameters to better leverage external knowledge or tools (e.g., documents or functions) through techniques like retrieval-augmented generation (RAG) and agent-based systems.

2 Detailed Outline

This will be a **three-hour** tutorial devoted to the **cutting-edge topic** of the adaptation of LLMs. Table 1 gives an overview.

1. **Introduction and Motivation**

1.1. **Challenges with General-purpose LLMs.** While LLMs have demonstrated strong generalization capabilities, they are general and static. They often fall short in highly specialized domains or tasks. These LLMs struggle to adapt to evolving requirements and exhibit high computational overhead due to their fixed nature. This section will highlight key limitations of them, with detailed examples and statistics to illustrate why adaptation is necessary for handling domain-specific or task-specific demands.

1.2. **Overview and Use Cases of LLM Adaptation.** LLM Adaptation adapts a pre-trained LLM to specialized use cases. It offers practical solutions for domain-specific applications, such as in finance and healthcare, as well as task-specific applications like retrieval-augmented generation and code generation. Personalized systems also benefit from adaptive models, which can fine-tune responses based on individual user needs. This section will showcase real-world use cases that demonstrate the critical need for LLM adaptability to address specialized scenarios.

1.3. **Key Concepts.** Before exploring detailed methodologies, we will introduce foundational concepts essential to understanding adaptive LLMs. These include distinctions between domain vs. task adaptation, continual learning vs. LLM adaptation, Parameter-Efficient Fine-Tuning (PEFT), different stages of post-training (e.g., Domain-Adaptive Pre-Training and Supervised Fine-Tuning), long-context LLMs, retrieval-augmented generation (RAG), agentic approach. These concepts will set the stage for the following technical sections.

1.4. **Research Questions in Data and Model Perspective.** In this tutorial, we aim to address several critical research questions. In data perspective, we focus on what gives a good data mixture and how to obtain high-quality data. In model perspective, we ask what constitutes an effective training recipe for adaptive LLMs, how can we properly evaluate adaptive models across different domains and tasks, what strategies can be used to prevent data leakage during post-training, and how can we scale up post-training efficiently. These questions will guide the subsequent discussions on evaluation and training.

2. **Evaluation and Benchmarks.** Evaluating adaptive LLMs involves a multidimensional approach. We will cover methods for assessing generalization, domain- and task-specific performance, and real-time effectiveness.

2.1. **General and Specialized Knowledge.** When adapting a model to specialize in specific knowledge, it is critical not to lose already learned general knowledge. A robust evaluation protocol should account for both. We will introduce methods to evaluate both types.

2.2. **Evaluation Metrics** . Numerous metrics have been discussed in the literature, such as perplexity, needle-in-haystack evaluations, and downstream task performance. We will compare and analyze the effectiveness of these metrics in evaluating adaptive LLMs.

3. **Parametric Knowledge Adaptation.** Multiple stages are undertaken to refine and specialize their knowledge for specific tasks and domains.

3.1. **Domain-Adaptive Pre-Training (DAPT).** Discuss the data and objective of DAPT that learn domain-specific background knowledge using raw text with next token prediction.
3.2. **Instruction Tuning (IT).** Discuss the data and objective of IT, also known as Supervised Fine-Tuning (SFT). It can be full model fine-tuning or parameter-efficient fine-tuning, with focus on instruction following ability.
3.3. **Preference Learning (PL)** Discuss the PL, where extra supervision on negative cases and delayed reward are introduced in this stage. The preference feedback can come from humans, AI models, or programmatic metrics. It can be done in online or offline (direct preference optimization; DPO) manner.
3.4. **Model Editing.** Discuss the techniques that allow for targeted updates in real-time, improving adaptability in production environments without the need for expensive retraining.

4. **Semi-parametric Knowledge Integration**

4.1. **Retrieval-augmented Generation (RAG)** How RAG allows models to dynamically retrieve external knowledge, and significantly enhance performance on specialized tasks or when up-to-date information is needed.
4.2. **Agent-based Integration.** This focuses more on the agentic aspect, highlighting the model as an agent that performs multi-step reasoning and interacts with external APIs and dynamic environments. It draws attention to the system's autonomous decision-making capacity and its ability to operate as an agent in complex environments.

5. **Summary, Discussion & QA**

3 Proportion of Other Researchers' Work, Reading list and Prerequisite

LLM adaptation involved almost all domains and tasks, making it become the main focus of industry and academic research. Our tutorial is designed to provide a comprehensive overview of this broad and rapidly evolving field, ensuring that the content reflects a wide range of techniques and contributions. As a result, the tutorial naturally includes a substantial amount of work from other researchers.

The prerequisite includes familiarity with basic knowledge of machine learning, NLP and LLM. Knowledge of continual learning is a plus. Here are a few papers that lay a foundation for this area and we encourage attendees to read the papers before the tutorial to familiarize themselves with foundational concepts and approaches:

- Continual pre-training of language models (Ke et al., 2023)
- Locating and editing factual associations in GPT (Meng et al., 2023a)
- Retrieval augmented language model pre-training (Guu et al., 2020)

Below, we provide a detailed reference to the works we plan to cover. While we will give pointers to dozens of relevant papers over the course of the tutorial, we plan to cover around 7-8 research papers in close detail. Only 1-2 of the "deep dive" papers will come from the presenter team.

Continual Learning learns a sequence of tasks sequentially without forgetting (Chen and Liu, 2018; McCloskey and Cohen, 1989; Van de Ven and Tolias, 2019; Mai et al., 2022; Aljundi et al., 2019; Ke and Liu, 2022), which is closely related to LLM adaptation. Typical approaches include *regularization-based methods* that regularize parameter updates to preserve important parameters (Kirkpatrick et al., 2016; Seff et al., 2017); *modular-based methods* that dynamically modify the architecture (Serrà et al., 2018; Wortsman et al., 2020); and *replay-based method* that recall previous experiences (Rebuffi et al., 2017; Wang et al., 2020).

Parametric Knowledge Adaptation adapts LLMs by updating its parametric knowledge. It has been widely adopted across board domains, such as code (Nijkamp et al., 2022), medical (Luo et al., 2023), law (Colombo et al., 2024), mathematics (Azerbayev et al., 2023), multi-lingual (Chen et al., 2024a) and finance (Ke et al., 2025; Xie et al., 2023a; Writer, 2024) and tasks such as function calling (Zhang et al., 2024b). Some focus on domain-specific or task-specific data curation (Yang et al., 2024b), mixture ratio (Que et al., 2024), data-efficiency (Xie et al., 2023b), hyperparameters (Parmar et al., 2024) or training recipe (Jiang et al., 2024; Yu et al., 2024; Gao et al., 2024).

Semi-Parametric Knowledge Adaptation augments LLMs with relevant information retrieved from various knowledge sources, i.e., RAG or external functions, i.e., agent-based intergation.

Retrieval-Augmented Generation (RAG) is proven effective across numerous NLP tasks, including language modeling (Borgeaud et al., 2022; Khandelwal et al., 2020; Shi et al., 2023), question answering (Ke et al., 2024; Lewis et al., 2020; Izacard et al., 2022; de Jong et al., 2023; De Jong et al., 2023; Shi et al., 2023; Guu et al., 2020; Izacard and Grave, 2020; Xu et al., 2023), fact versification (Lewis et al., 2020) and text generation (Lewis et al., 2020). Specifically, RAG utilizes input as a query and comprises two main components: a *retriever* retrieves a set of items from a side corpus, and a *LLM* incorporates the retrieved items, as additional information in the input context, and makes final predictions. Depending on which components are subject to updates, typical approaches can be categorized into three families: *adapting retrievers and LLMs jointly*, which is the most widely used setting of RAG (Izacard et al., 2022; Khandelwal et al., 2020; Wu et al., 2022; Guu et al., 2020; Lewis et al., 2020); *adapting LLMs only*, which avoid the costly updates of retrievers and document index (Izacard and Grave, 2020; De Jong et al., 2023; de Jong et al., 2023); and *adapting retrievers only*, which compatible with black-box LLMs (Shi et al., 2023; Xu et al., 2023).

Model Editing aims to adapt LLM in real-time without the need for expensive training or even without training (Zhang et al., 2024c; Wang et al., 2024). Typical approaches include *locate-and-edit* that first locate the position of the knowledge in LLMs and edit the KV cache (Meng et al., 2023a,b; Yang et al., 2024a; Gupta et al., 2024a,b), *meta-learning* that employ hyper-network to learn the editing (Tan et al., 2024; Cao et al., 2021; Mitchell et al., 2022) and *memory-based* that use memory elements to store and manipulate information during editing (Zhu et al., 2020; Ni et al., 2024; Zheng et al., 2023). As of now, editing is still in its infancy and suffers from serious forgetting, in particular when editing a sequence of samples.

Agent-based Integration augments the LLMs with external functions. Typical approaches include *fine-tuning the LLMs* for better function calling capacities (Qin et al., 2023; Chen et al., 2023; Patil et al., 2023; Zeng et al., 2023; Zhang et al., 2024a; Yin et al., 2024; Chen et al., 2024b; Li et al., 2023; Tang et al., 2023); and *prompting techniques* (Wei et al., 2023; Yao et al., 2022; Shinn et al., 2023)

4 Target Audience and Estimated Size

Researchers, graduate students, and practitioners who are interested in NLP and machine learning. The tutorial will is particularly beneficial to people who intend to develop machine learning and NLP techniques and applications that can adapt the LLM to specialized domains or tasks while preserving the original learned knowledge in the LLM. This tutorial has not been given before. Due to the increasing popularity of LLM and its adpatation, we estimate that there will be 100 to 150 people attending the tutorial.

5 Diversity Consideration

The topic of LLM adaptation will be inclusive for a broad range of communities. It will be of interest to industrial practitioners as they aim to deploy the best adaptive models for their targeted customers. Additionally, academic researchers will find value in this topic, as it essentially addresses a continual learning problem, enabling LLMs to adapt to new environments without forgetting—an essential step toward advancing Artificial General Intelligence. This topic also makes it easier for users to engage with LLMs, as it involves techniques to train smaller models that can be deployed efficiently. It naturally spans a wide range of domains and tasks, making it relevant to participants interested in various specific areas.

Our presenters include both junior and senior researchers from industry and academia, and we also bring geographical diversity, with instructors from both North America and Asia. This diverse group of instructors will help attract a wide audience and encourage participation from various backgrounds.

We will make our tutorial materials digitally accessible to all participants. All materials will be publicly available before the tutorial. We will provide slides and discussion questions before the tutorial to the audience. During the tutorial sessions, we will work with student volunteers to encourage open dialogue and promote active listening, allowing participants to share their thoughts and experiences without fear of judgment. After the tutorial, we will actively collect feedback to identify areas for improvement related to diversity and inclusion and share it with future tutorial presenters. Our presenter team will share our tutorial with a worldwide audience by promoting it on social media, and to diverse research communities. We will work with ACL/NAACL/EMNLP D&I teams, and consult resources such as the BIG directory to diversify our audience participation.

6 Ethics Statement

The tutorial will present general problems and algorithms related to LLM adaptation in NLP. All evaluation datasets are public domain benchmarks. Thus, the tutorial does not have any ethical issues.

7 Presenter Biography

Zixuan Ke is a research scientist at Salesforce AI Research, where he works with Dr. Shafiq Joty on continual pre-training of LLMs. Prior to that, he earned his Ph.D. at the University of Illinois, Chicago, where he worked with Dr. Bing Liu on continual learning. His research studies how to adapt the foundation models, particularly LLMs, for an ever-changing world characterized by emerging domains, events, topics, or information. He has published 25+ papers in top-tier conferences such as ICLR, ICML, NeurIPS, NAACL, ACL, and EMNLP with around 1.5K citations. He has served as an Area Chair and PC member for prestigious conferences such as ICLR, NeurIPS, ACL, EMNLP, and as a reviewer for leading journals such as Neural Networks, Neurocomputing, Artificial Intelligence, TKDE, and TPAMI, since 2021. He has given an invited short PhD course on continual learning at Aalborg University in the summer of 2022 and has also given several oral presentations at leading conferences. Further information about him, including past talks and slides, can be found at `https://vincent950129.github.io/`.

Yifei Ming is a Research Scientist at Salesforce AI Research. He received his Ph.D. in Computer Science from the University of Wisconsin-Madison in 2024. His research spans both empirical and theoretical studies, with a focus on understanding, benchmarking, and developing novel algorithms towards trustworthy foundation models (LLM and VLM). He has a prolific publication record with 20+ papers in top-tier AI conferences and journals. He co-organized several workshops and has served on the program committees of leading machine learning conferences and journals since 2021, including NeurIPS, ICLR, ICML, AAAI, EMNLP, IJCV, TPAMI, and NN. Further information can be found at `https://alvinmingsf.github.io/`.

Shafiq Joty is a research director at Salesforce Research and an Associate Professor at the Computer Science Department of the Nanyang Technological University. His research has contributed to over 30+ patents and 150+ papers in top-tier NLP and ML conferences and journals. He has served as a Program Chair of SIGDIAL'23, a member of the best paper award committees for ICLR'23 and NAACL'22, and in the capacity of a (senior) area chair for many leading NLP and ML conferences (e.g. NeurIPS, EMNLP, and ACL). He previously gave tutorials at EMNLP'23, IEEEVis'22, ACL'19, COLING'18 and ICDM'18. Further information about him, including past talks and slides, can be found at `https://raihanjoty.github.io/`.

References

Rahaf Aljundi, Min Lin, Baptiste Goujaud, and Yoshua Bengio. 2019. Gradient based sample selection for online continual learning. In *NeurIPS*.

Zhangir Azerbayev, Hailey Schoelkopf, Keiran Paster, Marco Dos Santos, Stephen McAleer, Albert Q Jiang, Jia Deng, Stella Biderman, and Sean Welleck. 2023. Llemma: An open language model for mathematics. *arXiv preprint arXiv:2310.10631*.

Sebastian Borgeaud, Arthur Mensch, Jordan Hoffmann, Trevor Cai, Eliza Rutherford, Katie Millican, George Bm Van Den Driessche, Jean-Baptiste Lespiau, Bogdan Damoc, Aidan Clark, et al. 2022. Improving language models by retrieving from trillions of tokens. In *International conference on machine learning*, pages 2206–2240. PMLR.

Nicola De Cao, Wilker Aziz, and Ivan Titov. 2021. Editing factual knowledge in language models.

Baian Chen, Chang Shu, Ehsan Shareghi, Nigel Collier, Karthik Narasimhan, and Shunyu Yao. 2023. Fireact: Toward language agent fine-tuning.

Jie Chen, Zhipeng Chen, Jiapeng Wang, Kun Zhou, Yutao Zhu, Jinhao Jiang, Yingqian Min, Wayne Xin Zhao, Zhicheng Dou, Jiaxin Mao, Yankai Lin, Ruihua Song, Jun Xu, Xu Chen, Rui Yan, Zhewei Wei, Di Hu, Wenbing Huang, and Ji-Rong Wen. 2024a. Towards effective and efficient continual pre-training of large language models.

Zehui Chen, Kuikun Liu, Qiuchen Wang, Wenwei Zhang, Jiangning Liu, Dahua Lin, Kai Chen, and Feng Zhao. 2024b. Agent-flan: Designing data and methods of effective agent tuning for large language models.

Zhiyuan Chen and Bing Liu. 2018. Lifelong machine learning. *Synthesis Lectures on Artificial Intelligence and Machine Learning*, 12(3).

Pierre Colombo, Telmo Pessoa Pires, Malik Boudiaf, Dominic Culver, Rui Melo, Caio Corro, Andre FT Martins, Fabrizio Esposito, Vera Lúcia Raposo, Sofia Morgado, et al. 2024. Saullm-7b: A pioneering large language model for law. *arXiv preprint arXiv:2403.03883*.

Michiel De Jong, Yury Zemlyanskiy, Nicholas FitzGerald, Joshua Ainslie, Sumit Sanghai, Fei Sha, and William W Cohen. 2023. Pre-computed memory or on-the-fly encoding? a hybrid approach to retrieval augmentation makes the most of your compute. In *International Conference on Machine Learning*, pages 7329–7342. PMLR.

Michiel de Jong, Yury Zemlyanskiy, Nicholas FitzGerald, Sumit Sanghai, William W Cohen, and Joshua Ainslie. 2023. Glimmer: generalized late-interaction memory reranker. *arXiv preprint arXiv:2306.10231*.

Tianyu Gao, Alexander Wettig, Howard Yen, and Danqi Chen. 2024. How to train long-context language models (effectively).

Akshat Gupta, Sidharth Baskaran, and Gopala Anumanchipalli. 2024a. Rebuilding rome : Resolving model collapse during sequential model editing.

Akshat Gupta, Dev Sajnani, and Gopala Anumanchipalli. 2024b. A unified framework for model editing.

Kelvin Guu, Kenton Lee, Zora Tung, Panupong Pasupat, and Mingwei Chang. 2020. Retrieval augmented language model pre-training. In *International conference on machine learning*, pages 3929–3938. PMLR.

Gautier Izacard and Edouard Grave. 2020. Leveraging passage retrieval with generative models for open domain question answering. *arXiv preprint arXiv:2007.01282*.

Gautier Izacard, Patrick Lewis, Maria Lomeli, Lucas Hosseini, Fabio Petroni, Timo Schick, Jane Dwivedi-Yu, Armand Joulin, Sebastian Riedel, and Edouard Grave. 2022. Few-shot learning with retrieval augmented language models. *arXiv preprint arXiv:2208.03299*.

Zhengbao Jiang, Zhiqing Sun, Weijia Shi, Pedro Rodriguez, Chunting Zhou, Graham Neubig, Xi Victoria Lin, Wen-tau Yih, and Srinivasan Iyer. 2024. Instruction-tuned language models are better knowledge learners. *arXiv preprint arXiv:2402.12847*.

Zixuan Ke, Weize Kong, Cheng Li, Mingyang Zhang, Qiaozhu Mei, and Michael Bendersky. 2024. Bridging the preference gap between retrievers and llms. *arXiv preprint arXiv:2401.06954*.

Zixuan Ke and Bing Liu. 2022. Continual learning of natural language processing tasks: A survey. In *Arkiv*.

Zixuan Ke, Yifei Ming, Xuan-Phi Nguyen, Caiming Xiong, and Shafiq Joty. 2025. Demystifying domain-adaptive post-training for financial llms. *arXiv preprint arXiv:2501.04961*.

Zixuan Ke, Yijia Shao, Haowei Lin, Tatsuya Konishi, Gyuhak Kim, and Bing Liu. 2023. Continual pre-training of language models. *arXiv preprint arXiv:2302.03241*.

Urvashi Khandelwal, Omer Levy, Dan Jurafsky, Luke Zettlemoyer, and Mike Lewis. 2020. Generalization through memorization: Nearest neighbor language models. In *International Conference on Learning Representations*.

James Kirkpatrick, Razvan Pascanu, Neil C. Rabinowitz, Joel Veness, Guillaume Desjardins, Andrei A. Rusu, Kieran Milan, John Quan, Tiago Ramalho, Agnieszka Grabska-Barwinska, Demis Hassabis, Claudia Clopath, Dharshan Kumaran, and Raia Hadsell. 2016. Overcoming catastrophic forgetting in neural networks. *CoRR*.

Patrick Lewis, Ethan Perez, Aleksandra Piktus, Fabio Petroni, Vladimir Karpukhin, Naman Goyal, Heinrich Küttler, Mike Lewis, Wen-tau Yih, Tim Rocktäschel, et al. 2020. Retrieval-augmented generation for knowledge-intensive nlp tasks. *Advances in Neural Information Processing Systems*, 33:9459–9474.

Minghao Li, Yingxiu Zhao, Bowen Yu, Feifan Song, Hangyu Li, Haiyang Yu, Zhoujun Li, Fei Huang, and Yongbin Li. 2023. API-bank: A comprehensive benchmark for tool-augmented LLMs. In *Proceedings of the 2023 Conference on Empirical Methods in Natural Language Processing*.

Yizhen Luo, Jiahuan Zhang, Siqi Fan, Kai Yang, Yushuai Wu, Mu Qiao, and Zaiqing Nie. 2023. Biomedgpt: Open multimodal generative pre-trained transformer for biomedicine. *arXiv preprint arXiv:2308.09442*.

Zheda Mai, Ruiwen Li, Jihwan Jeong, David Quispe, Hyunwoo Kim, and Scott Sanner. 2022. Online continual learning in image classification: An empirical survey. *Neurocomputing*, 469.

Nestor Maslej, Loredana Fattorini, Raymond Perrault, Vanessa Parli, Anka Reuel, Erik Brynjolfsson, John Etchemendy, Katrina Ligett, Terah Lyons, James Manyika, Juan Carlos Niebles, Yoav Shoham, Russell Wald, and Jack Clark. 2024. The ai index 2024 annual report,.

Michael McCloskey and Neal J Cohen. 1989. Catastrophic interference in connectionist networks: The sequential learning problem. In *Psychology of learning and motivation*.

Kevin Meng, David Bau, Alex Andonian, and Yonatan Belinkov. 2023a. Locating and editing factual associations in gpt.

Kevin Meng, Arnab Sen Sharma, Alex Andonian, Yonatan Belinkov, and David Bau. 2023b. Mass-editing memory in a transformer.

Eric Mitchell, Charles Lin, Antoine Bosselut, Chelsea Finn, and Christopher D. Manning. 2022. Fast model editing at scale.

Shiwen Ni, Dingwei Chen, Chengming Li, Xiping Hu, Ruifeng Xu, and Min Yang. 2024. Forgetting before learning: Utilizing parametric arithmetic for knowledge updating in large language models.

Erik Nijkamp, Bo Pang, Hiroaki Hayashi, Lifu Tu, Huan Wang, Yingbo Zhou, Silvio Savarese, and Caiming Xiong. 2022. Codegen: An open large language model for code with multi-turn program synthesis. *arXiv preprint arXiv:2203.13474*.

Jupinder Parmar, Sanjev Satheesh, Mostofa Patwary, Mohammad Shoeybi, and Bryan Catanzaro. 2024. Reuse, don't retrain: A recipe for continued pre-training of language models. *arXiv preprint arXiv:2407.07263*.

Shishir G. Patil, Tianjun Zhang, Xin Wang, and Joseph E. Gonzalez. 2023. Gorilla: Large language model connected with massive apis.

Yujia Qin, Shihao Liang, Yining Ye, Kunlun Zhu, Lan Yan, Yaxi Lu, Yankai Lin, Xin Cong, Xiangru Tang, Bill Qian, Sihan Zhao, Lauren Hong, Runchu Tian, Ruobing Xie, Jie Zhou, Mark Gerstein, Dahai Li, Zhiyuan Liu, and Maosong Sun. 2023. Toolllm: Facilitating large language models to master 16000+ real-world apis.

Haoran Que, Jiaheng Liu, Ge Zhang, Chenchen Zhang, Xingwei Qu, Yinghao Ma, Feiyu Duan, Zhiqi Bai, Jiakai Wang, Yuanxing Zhang, Xu Tan, Jie Fu, Wenbo Su, Jiamang Wang, Lin Qu, and Bo Zheng. 2024. D-cpt law: Domain-specific continual pre-training scaling law for large language models.

Sylvestre-Alvise Rebuffi, Alexander Kolesnikov, Georg Sperl, and Christoph H. Lampert. 2017. icarl: Incremental classifier and representation learning. In *CVPR*.

Ari Seff, Alex Beatson, Daniel Suo, and Han Liu. 2017. Continual learning in generative adversarial nets. *CoRR*, abs/1705.08395.

Joan Serrà, Didac Suris, Marius Miron, and Alexandros Karatzoglou. 2018. Overcoming catastrophic forgetting with hard attention to the task. In *ICML*.

Weijia Shi, Sewon Min, Michihiro Yasunaga, Minjoon Seo, Rich James, Mike Lewis, Luke Zettlemoyer, and Wen-tau Yih. 2023. Replug: Retrieval-augmented black-box language models. *arXiv preprint arXiv:2301.12652*.

Noah Shinn, Beck Labash, and Ashwin Gopinath. 2023. Reflexion: an autonomous agent with dynamic memory and self-reflection. *arXiv preprint arXiv:2303.11366*.

Chenmien Tan, Ge Zhang, and Jie Fu. 2024. Massive editing for large language models via meta learning.

Qiaoyu Tang, Ziliang Deng, Hongyu Lin, Xianpei Han, Qiao Liang, Boxi Cao, and Le Sun. 2023. Toolalpaca: Generalized tool learning for language models with 3000 simulated cases.

Gido M Van de Ven and Andreas S Tolias. 2019. Three scenarios for continual learning. *arXiv preprint arXiv:1904.07734*.

Song Wang, Yaochen Zhu, Haochen Liu, Zaiyi Zheng, Chen Chen, and Jundong Li. 2024. Knowledge editing for large language models: A survey.

Zirui Wang, Sanket Vaibhav Mehta, Barnabás Póczos, and Jaime Carbonell. 2020. Efficient meta lifelong-learning with limited memory. In *EMNLP*.

Jason Wei, Xuezhi Wang, Dale Schuurmans, Maarten Bosma, Brian Ichter, Fei Xia, Ed Chi, Quoc Le, and Denny Zhou. 2023. Chain-of-thought prompting elicits reasoning in large language models.

Mitchell Wortsman, Vivek Ramanujan, Rosanne Liu, Aniruddha Kembhavi, Mohammad Rastegari, Jason Yosinski, and Ali Farhadi. 2020. Supermasks in superposition. In *NeurIPS*.

Writer. 2024. Palmyra-Fin-70B-32k: a powerful LLM designed for Finance. `https://dev.writer.com`.

Yuhuai Wu, Markus N Rabe, DeLesley Hutchins, and Christian Szegedy. 2022. Memorizing transformers. *arXiv preprint arXiv:2203.08913*.

Qianqian Xie, Weiguang Han, Xiao Zhang, Yanzhao Lai, Min Peng, Alejandro Lopez-Lira, and Jimin Huang. 2023a. Pixiu: A large language model, instruction data and evaluation benchmark for finance.

Yong Xie, Karan Aggarwal, and Aitzaz Ahmad. 2023b. Efficient continual pre-training for building domain specific large language models.

Fangyuan Xu, Weijia Shi, and Eunsol Choi. 2023. Recomp: Improving retrieval-augmented lms with compression and selective augmentation. *arXiv preprint arXiv:2310.04408*.

Wanli Yang, Fei Sun, Xinyu Ma, Xun Liu, Dawei Yin, and Xueqi Cheng. 2024a. The butterfly effect of model editing: Few edits can trigger large language models collapse.

Zitong Yang, Neil Band, Shuangping Li, Emmanuel Candès, and Tatsunori Hashimoto. 2024b. Synthetic continued pretraining. *arXiv preprint arXiv:2409.07431*.

Shunyu Yao, Jeffrey Zhao, Dian Yu, Nan Du, Izhak Shafran, Karthik Narasimhan, and Yuan Cao. 2022. React: Synergizing reasoning and acting in language models. *arXiv preprint arXiv:2210.03629*.

Da Yin, Faeze Brahman, Abhilasha Ravichander, Khyathi Chandu, Kai-Wei Chang, Yejin Choi, and Bill Yuchen Lin. 2024. Agent lumos: Unified and modular training for open-source language agents.

Xiao Yu, Qingyang Wu, Yu Li, and Zhou Yu. 2024. Lions: An empirically optimized approach to align language models.

Aohan Zeng, Mingdao Liu, Rui Lu, Bowen Wang, Xiao Liu, Yuxiao Dong, and Jie Tang. 2023. Agenttuning: Enabling generalized agent abilities for llms.

Jianguo Zhang, Tian Lan, Rithesh Murthy, Zhiwei Liu, Weiran Yao, Juntao Tan, Thai Hoang, Liangwei Yang, Yihao Feng, Zuxin Liu, Tulika Awalgaonkar, Juan Carlos Niebles, Silvio Savarese,

Shelby Heinecke, Huan Wang, and Caiming Xiong. 2024a. Agentohana: Design unified data and training pipeline for effective agent learning.

Jianguo Zhang, Tian Lan, Ming Zhu, Zuxin Liu, Thai Hoang, Shirley Kokane, Weiran Yao, Juntao Tan, Akshara Prabhakar, Haolin Chen, et al. 2024b. xlam: A family of large action models to empower ai agent systems. *arXiv preprint arXiv:2409.03215*.

Ningyu Zhang, Yunzhi Yao, Bozhong Tian, Peng Wang, Shumin Deng, Mengru Wang, Zekun Xi, Shengyu Mao, Jintian Zhang, Yuansheng Ni, Siyuan Cheng, Ziwen Xu, Xin Xu, Jia-Chen Gu, Yong Jiang, Pengjun Xie, Fei Huang, Lei Liang, Zhiqiang Zhang, Xiaowei Zhu, Jun Zhou, and Huajun Chen. 2024c. A comprehensive study of knowledge editing for large language models.

Ce Zheng, Lei Li, Qingxiu Dong, Yuxuan Fan, Zhiyong Wu, Jingjing Xu, and Baobao Chang. 2023. Can we edit factual knowledge by in-context learning?

Chen Zhu, Ankit Singh Rawat, Manzil Zaheer, Srinadh Bhojanapalli, Daliang Li, Felix Yu, and Sanjiv Kumar. 2020. Modifying memories in transformer models.

Learning Language through Grounding

Freda Shi[1,2] **Ziqiao Ma**[3] **Jiayuan Mao**[4] **Parisa Kordjamshidi**[5] **Joyce Chai**[3]
[1]University of Waterloo [2]Vector Institute & Canada CIFAR AI Chair [3]University of Michigan
[4]Massachusetts Institute of Technology [5]Michigan State University
fhs@uwaterloo.ca, {marstin,chaijy}@umich.edu
jiayuanm@mit.edu, kordjams@msu.edu

Abstract

Grounding has been a long-standing concept in natural language processing (NLP) and computational linguistics (CL). This tutorial provides a historical overview and introduces recent advances in learning language through grounding, with a particular emphasis on the latter. We will begin by tracing the history of grounding and presenting a unified perspective on the term. In Parts II to IV, we will delve into recent progress in learning lexical semantics, syntax, and complex meanings through various forms of grounding. We will conclude by discussing future directions and open challenges, particularly those related to the growing trend of large language models and scaling.

1 Introduction

Humans can learn and use language efficiently and effectively. Importantly, human language acquisition, learning, and use are *grounded* to contexts in the world, drawing on information from various sensory modalities such as visual and auditory signals, as well as interactions with other people and the surrounding physical environment. To better understand human language learning and build intelligent language agents, modeling language acquisition and learning has been a long-term interest in the fields of computational linguistics (CL) and natural language processing (NLP), drawing cross-disciplinary interest from fields such as cognitive science and robotics (Steels et al., 2000; Steels, 2003). Recently, we have all witnessed that advances in machine learning, especially those driven by large-scale multimodal data, have significantly advanced the field of grounded language learning (Kiros et al., 2014; Tan and Bansal, 2019; Radford et al., 2021, *inter alia*).

Although language grounding has emerged as a promising direction in language understanding research and is drawing growing attention from the CL and NLP community (Bisk et al., 2020), the usage of the term *grounding* has diverged (Chai et al., 2018). Two major lines of work on grounding started almost contemporaneously in different areas: [1; semantic grounding] in artificial intelligence (AI), which refers to connecting language units to the world that gives language meanings (Harnad, 1990), and [2; communicative grounding] in psychology, which means finding common ground between agents in a communication setting (Clark and Brennan, 1991). Given the interdisciplinary nature and rapid advancement of CL and NLP, especially driven by the emerging trend of language models and scaling, the convergence of various fields has made it imperative to re-examine the concept of grounding in the current context.

This tutorial will start by reviewing the evolution of the concept of grounding in the literature and introduce a unified view of grounding (Shi, 2024). After that, we will introduce recent work on computational approaches that model the acquisition and learning of natural language by grounding natural language to the world, including learning lexical semantics, syntax, complex forms of semantics, and pragmatics in various grounded settings. The tutorial will conclude with a discussion of future directions and open problems in the field, particularly regarding the emerging trend of language models and scaling.

Tutorial type. This tutorial should be classified as *cutting-edge* in CL/NLP, as most of the content was introduced within the last ten years; however, it will also include introductory content that familiarizes the audience with the necessary backgrounds.

Related tutorials. There have been two *ACL tutorials focusing on communicative grounding, i.e., building common ground through dialogue communications (Alikhani and Stone, 2020; Krishnaswamy and Pustejovsky, 2022); in contrast, this tutorial will (1) place greater emphasis on semantic grounding when introducing exemplar work and (2) delve deeper into the pragmatic aspects of

Proceedings of the 2025 Annual Conference of the Nations of the Americas Chapter of the Association for Computational Linguistics: Human Language Technologies: Tutorial Abstracts, pages 38–43

language use in communicative grounding, which has not been explicitly mentioned in previous tutorials. Additionally, while a related NAACL tutorial by a member of the instructor team introduces spatial and temporal language understanding (Kordjamshidi et al., 2024), this tutorial will offer a broader overview of the grounded language learning problems in general.

Target audience. This tutorial aims to attract a broad audience. We expect that the tutorial will be of interest to researchers and students in CL/NLP, particularly those who are interested in multimodal machine learning and grounded language learning. We expect the audience to understand basic concepts in calculus (derivatives and calculus), linear algebra (matrix, linear transformation), probability (probability distribution, expectation, and variance), and statistics (sampling from a distribution). Familiarity with neural networks, common practices in deep learning, and basic linguistic concepts is desired but not required.

2 Outline of Tutorial Content

We anticipate that the tutorial will be about 3 hours long. After an introduction to grounding, we break down the tutorial with respect to particular learning objectives.

- **Part I** (20 minutes): Introduction to grounding. We will review the history of grounding (Harnad, 1990; Clark and Brennan, 1991; Chai et al., 2018), and introduce the unified definition of grounding (Shi, 2024). In particular, grounding, in this tutorial, refers to processing the primary data with supervision from another source, where the two sources of data have positive mutual information. We will exemplify the definition through connection to existing work such as visual grounding (e.g., Kiros et al., 2014), acoustic grounding (e.g., Settle et al., 2019), factual grounding (e.g., Ghazvininejad et al., 2018), and cross-lingual grounding (e.g., Chen et al., 2021). We refer to Alikhani and Stone (2020) for building common ground through communication.

- **Part II** (30 minutes): Learning lexicons through grounding. Word acquisition has been a fundamental problem in language acquisition concerned by both cognitive sciences (Siskind, 1996; Roy and Pentland, 2002; Xu and Tenenbaum, 2007; Qu and Chai, 2010, *inter alia*) and robotics (Steels et al., 2000; Steels, 2003). With the advancement of neural networks and multimodal machine learning, there has been work on learning the meanings of written (Forbes and Choi, 2017; Mao et al., 2019; Ma et al., 2023) or spoken (Peng and Harwath, 2022) words by grounding language to visual signals. Particularly, there has been work focusing on grounding verb semantics to the change of the physical world (Gao et al., 2016; She and Chai, 2016, 2017). Another line of work on learning lexicons through cross-lingual grounding can be exemplified by Chen et al. (2021).

  In the first 10 minutes, we will introduce the background and focus on recent advances in the remaining time. Work on learning lexical semantics through interaction (Wang et al., 2016) or learning lexicon to compose sentence-level meanings (Mao et al., 2021) will be deferred to Part IV.

- **Part III** (30 minutes): Learning syntax through grounding. As shown by Shi et al. (2019), constituency parses of sentences can be learned by grounding to visual signals. Follow-up work has demonstrated the effectiveness of such visually grounded systems on learning variants of constituency (Kojima et al., 2020; Zhao and Titov, 2020; Zhang et al., 2021; Lai et al., 2023; Portelance et al., 2024) and dependency (Su et al., 2021) grammars. On another line, word alignment–based cross-lingual transfer can also be considered as an instantiation of learning syntax through cross-lingual grounding (Ma and Xia, 2014; Rasooli et al., 2021; Kurniawan et al., 2021, *inter alia*), where the text in the target language(s) is grounded to existing knowledge in the source language(s).

  A brief introduction of related syntactic knowledge, such as constituency (Chomsky, 1957), dependency (Tesnière, 1959), and combinatory categorial grammars (CCGs; Steedman, 2000), will be presented in the first 10 minutes of this part to help the audience better understand the content. We will focus on recent approaches to learning syntax through visual grounding and cross-lingual grounding in the rest of the time. Efforts on joint learning of syntax and semantics (e.g., Mao et al., 2021) will be delivered in Part IV.

- **Part IV** (60 minutes): Learning complex meanings, e.g., semantics and pragmatics, through grounding. It has attracted significant interest in learning (Kiros et al., 2014; Tan and Bansal,

2020; Mao et al., 2021, *inter alia*) and evaluating (Antol et al., 2015; Suhr et al., 2017; Kordjamshidi et al., 2017; Lake and Baroni, 2018; Mirzaee et al., 2021, *inter alia*) meaning acquisition in visually grounded settings. In addition to visual grounding, interaction is also a common source of supervision, where considerations regarding pragmatics and theory of mind are often taken into account (Wang et al., 2016; Yu et al., 2020; Zhu et al., 2022; Liu et al., 2023; Ou et al., 2023). Similarly to what has been mentioned in Part II, cross-lingual transfer on sentence or document-level meanings, particularly transferring knowledge from high-resource to low-resource languages, should also be considered as instantiations of cross-lingual grounding (Artetxe et al., 2020; Tran et al., 2020; Shi et al., 2023, *inter alia*).

This part will cover three topics for 20 minutes each: learning semantics through grounding, learning pragmatics through grounded interaction, and learning cross-lingual text representations through cross-lingual grounding.

- **Part V** (15 minutes): Discussion on future directions and open problems. A key discussion for future directions centers around whether grounding should emerge naturally from scaling models or whether we should enforce grounded supervision to achieve more efficient learning. Additionally, the scope of grounding can be broadened beyond traditional modalities, incorporating touch, olfaction, non-human sensors, video and temporal data, 3D environments, proprioception, episodic experiences, and even other forms of meta-cognition.

There will be a 5-minute Q&A session at the end of each part to address questions from the audience. A 30-minute coffee break will be held after Part III. We anticipate that 30% of the tutorial content will be work by at least one of the instructors, with the rest coming from other research groups.

2.1 Recommended Reading List

All readings below are optional; however, reading the materials listed below in advance will help the audience understand the tutorial content better.

We recommend Harnad (1990) and Clark and Brennan (1991) as background knowledge, as well as Chai et al. (2018) and Chapter 2 of Shi (2024) for an introduction to grounded language learning in a recent context. For audiences interested in more comprehensive surveys of recent work on language grounding, we recommend Bisk et al. (2020) for a roadmap and Chandu et al. (2021) for why communicative grounding has been overlooked.

Regarding background knowledge about linguistic structures, we recommend Chapters 6, 18, 19, and 21 of Jurafsky and Martin (2024), as well as Steedman (2000) for audiences interested in gaining a deeper understanding of CCGs.

For parts II-IV, we will refer the audience to the cited articles above in the tutorial outline. We encourage the audience to use the papers mentioned above as "pointers" to more comprehensive literature, which can be accessed through papers citing or cited by these aforementioned ones.

3 Specification of the Tutorial

Diversity considerations. This tutorial promotes diversity from the following aspects:

- **Topic diversity.** Language grounding is inherently a multidisciplinary field that intersects linguistics, machine learning, computer vision, robotics, cognitive science, and social science.
- **Linguistic diversity.** This tutorial will promote linguistic diversity in the NLP community. A key aspect of grounded language learning is cross-lingual grounding, which has been extensively explored in recent research, and the tutorial will cover a significant amount of work on cross-lingual grounding. In particular, much of the covered work in this tutorial has significantly contributed to low-resource NLP.
- **Diverse representation in the instructor team.** Our instructor team represents a diverse range of backgrounds, including various seniority levels, demographic backgrounds, home institutions, and geolocations.
- **Effort on participation diversity.** We are committed to making the tutorial content accessible to a broad audience with diverse academic backgrounds by ensuring that the fundamental concepts are thoroughly covered in the released tutorial material. Upon acceptance, we will invest efforts on encouraging everyone in the CL/NLP community to participate, especially those from a historically underrepresented group.

Estimated audience size. Given that cross-lingual NLP and cross-modal machine learning have been popular research topics in recent years and that the tutorial will cover a wide range of topics in grounded language learning, we expect around 200 in-person attendees.

Technical equipment. We have no major technical requirements beyond the basic settings of conference tutorials: we will need a projector, a screen, and a microphone. Connection to the Internet is strongly preferred but not required.

Ethics statement. Learning language through grounding involves the use of human language and multimodal data, which may raise ethical concerns in terms of data privacy and fairness. We will emphasize related ethical considerations in the tutorial, including the importance of data privacy, the potential biases in data used in relevant research, and the common practices in the field to mitigate negative impacts. All tutorial material will be made publicly available after the tutorial.

4 Tutorial Instructors

Freda Shi is an Assistant Professor at the University of Waterloo and a Faculty Member at the Vector Institute, where she holds a Canada CIFAR AI Chair position. Her research interests are in the intersection of natural language processing, with a focus on grounded language learning. Her work has been recognized with a Google PhD Fellowship, and several nominations for the Best Paper Award at ACL. Her doctoral dissertation entitled *Learning Language Structures through Grounding* focuses on learning syntactic and semantic structures through grounding language to various modalities that represent the real world. She has given invited talks on grounded language learning, syntactic parsing, and multilingual NLP at more than ten institutions in multiple countries.

Ziqiao Ma is a Ph.D. candidate at the University of Michigan. His research stands on the intersection of language, interaction, and embodiment from a cognitive perspective, with the goal of grounding and aligning language agents to non-linguistic modalities and rich interactive contexts. He received the Weinberg Cognitive Science Fellowship, an Outstanding Paper Award at ACL 2023, and the Amazon Alexa Prize Simbot Challenge Award. He co-organized the SpLU-RoboNLP workshop at ACL 2024, Bi-Align workshop at ICLR 2025. He has instructed NLP/AI courses three times, and has delivered guest lectures and invited talks on situated language processing and grounded and interactive language learning at multiple institutions worldwide.

Jiayuan Mao is a Ph.D. student at MIT, advised by Professors Josh Tenenbaum and Leslie Kaelbling. Her research agenda is to build machines that can continually learn concepts (e.g., properties, relations, rules, and skills) from their experiences and apply them for reasoning and planning in the physical world. Her research topics include visual reasoning, robotic manipulation, scene and activity understanding, and language acquisition. Her work is supported by an MIT presidential fellowship. She has co-organized the Workshop on Planning in the Era of LLMs at AAAI 2024, the Workshop on Learning Effective Abstractions for Planning at CoRL 2024, the Workshop on Visual Concepts at ECCV 2024, the workshop on Visually Grounded Interaction and Language (ViGIL) at NAACL 2021, and the Neuro-Symbolic Visual Reasoning and Program Synthesis tutorial at CVPR 2020.

Parisa Kordjamshidi is an Associate Professor at the CSE Department, Michigan State University. She has worked on spatial language understanding, language grounding, and a variety of vision and language problems. She organized shared tasks on Spatial role labeling, SpRL-2012, SpRL-2013, the Space Evaluation workshop, SpaceEval-2015 in SemEval Series, Multimodal spatial role labeling workshop (MSpRL) at CLEF-2017. She co-organized SpLU-2018, SpLU-RoboNLP-2019, SpLU-2020, SpLU-2021, and SpLU-RoboNLP-2024 workshops collocated with NAACL, EMNLP and ACL. She has given tutorials on spatial and temporal language understanding at NAACL 2024 and COLING 2022.

Joyce Chai is a Professor in the Department of Electrical Engineering and Computer Science at the University of Michigan. Her research interests span NLP and embodied AI to human-AI collaboration. Her current work explores the intersection between language, perception, and action to enable situated communication with embodied agents. She served on the executive board of NAACL and as a Program Co-Chair for multiple conferences, most recently ACL 2020. She is a recipient of the NSF CAREER Award and multiple paper awards with her students (e.g., Best Long Paper Award at ACL 2010, Outstanding Paper Awards at EMNLP 2021 and ACL 2023). Her lab (the SEAGULL team) won the first prize in Amazon Alexa Simbot Challenge in 2023. She is a Fellow of ACL.

References

Malihe Alikhani and Matthew Stone. 2020. Achieving common ground in multi-modal dialogue. In *ACL*.

Stanislaw Antol, Aishwarya Agrawal, Jiasen Lu, Margaret Mitchell, Dhruv Batra, C Lawrence Zitnick, and Devi Parikh. 2015. VQA: Visual question answering. In *ICCV*.

Mikel Artetxe, Sebastian Ruder, and Dani Yogatama. 2020. On the cross-lingual transferability of monolingual representations. In *ACL*.

Yonatan Bisk, Ari Holtzman, Jesse Thomason, Jacob Andreas, Yoshua Bengio, Joyce Chai, Mirella Lapata, Angeliki Lazaridou, Jonathan May, Aleksandr Nisnevich, Nicolas Pinto, and Joseph Turian. 2020. Experience grounds language. In *EMNLP*.

Joyce Y. Chai, Qiaozi Gao, Lanbo She, Shaohua Yang, Sari Saba-Sadiya, and Guangyue Xu. 2018. Language to action: Towards interactive task learning with physical agents. In *IJCAI*.

Khyathi Raghavi Chandu, Yonatan Bisk, and Alan W. Black. 2021. Grounding 'grounding' in nlp. In *Findings of ACL*.

Muhao Chen, Weijia Shi, Ben Zhou, and Dan Roth. 2021. Cross-lingual entity alignment with incidental supervision. In *EACL*.

Noam Chomsky. 1957. *Syntactic Structures*. Mouton & Co.

Herbert H. Clark and Susan E. Brennan. 1991. Grounding in communication. *Perspectives on socially shared cognition*, pages 127–149.

Maxwell Forbes and Yejin Choi. 2017. Verb physics: Relative physical knowledge of actions and objects. In *ACL*.

Qiaozi Gao, Malcolm Doering, Shaohua Yang, and Joyce Chai. 2016. Physical causality of action verbs in grounded language understanding. In *ACL*.

Marjan Ghazvininejad, Chris Brockett, Ming-Wei Chang, Bill Dolan, Jianfeng Gao, Wen-tau Yih, and Michel Galley. 2018. A knowledge-grounded neural conversation model. In *AAAI*.

Stevan Harnad. 1990. The symbol grounding problem. *Physica D: Nonlinear Phenomena*, 42(1-3):335–346.

Daniel Jurafsky and James H. Martin. 2024. *Speech and Language Processing (3rd ed.)*. Prentice Hall.

Ryan Kiros, Ruslan Salakhutdinov, and Richard S. Zemel. 2014. Unifying visual-semantic embeddings with multimodal neural language models. *arXiv preprint arXiv:1411.2539*.

Noriyuki Kojima, Hadar Averbuch-Elor, Alexander Rush, and Yoav Artzi. 2020. What is learned in visually grounded neural syntax acquisition. In *ACL*.

Parisa Kordjamshidi, Qiang Ning, James Pustejovsky, and Marie-Francine Moens. 2024. Spatial and temporal language understanding: Representation, reasoning, and grounding. In *NAACL*.

Parisa Kordjamshidi, Martijn van Otterlo, and Marie-Francine Moens. 2017. Spatial role labeling annotation scheme. *Handbook of linguistic annotation*, pages 1025–1052.

Nikhil Krishnaswamy and James Pustejovsky. 2022. Grounding meaning representation for situated reasoning. In *AACL*.

Kemal Kurniawan, Lea Frermann, Philip Schulz, and Trevor Cohn. 2021. PPT: Parsimonious parser transfer for unsupervised cross-lingual adaptation. In *EACL*.

Cheng-I Jeff Lai, Freda Shi, Puyuan Peng, Yoon Kim, Kevin Gimpel, Shiyu Chang, Yung-Sung Chuang, Saurabhchand Bhati, David Cox, David Harwath, Yang Zhang, Karen Livescu, and James Glass. 2023. Audio-visual neural syntax acquisition. In *ASRU*.

Brenden Lake and Marco Baroni. 2018. Generalization without systematicity: On the compositional skills of sequence-to-sequence recurrent networks. In *ICML*.

Andy Liu, Hao Zhu, Emmy Liu, Yonatan Bisk, and Graham Neubig. 2023. Computational language acquisition with theory of mind. In *ICLR*.

Xuezhe Ma and Fei Xia. 2014. Unsupervised dependency parsing with transferring distribution via parallel guidance and entropy regularization. In *ACL*.

Ziqiao Ma, Jiayi Pan, and Joyce Chai. 2023. World-to-words: Grounded open vocabulary acquisition through fast mapping in vision-language models. In *ACL*.

Jiayuan Mao, Chuang Gan, Pushmeet Kohli, Joshua B. Tenenbaum, and Jiajun Wu. 2019. The Neuro-Symbolic Concept Learner: Interpreting Scenes, Words, and Sentences From Natural Supervision. In *ICLR*.

Jiayuan Mao, Freda Shi, Jiajun Wu, Roger P. Levy, and Joshua B. Tenenbaum. 2021. Grammar-based grounded lexicon learning. In *NeurIPS*.

Roshanak Mirzaee, Hossein Rajaby Faghihi, Qiang Ning, and Parisa Kordjamshidi. 2021. Spartqa: A textual question answering benchmark for spatial reasoning. In *NAACL-HLT*.

Jiefu Ou, Benno Krojer, and Daniel Fried. 2023. Pragmatic inference with a clip listener for contrastive captioning. In *Findings of ACL*.

Puyuan Peng and David Harwath. 2022. Word discovery in visually grounded, self-supervised speech models. In *Interspeech*.

Eva Portelance, Siva Reddy, and Timothy J O'Donnell. 2024. Reframing linguistic bootstrapping as joint inference using visually-grounded grammar induction models. *arXiv:2406.11977*.

Shaolin Qu and Joyce Yue Chai. 2010. Context-based word acquisition for situated dialogue in a virtual world. *Journal of Artificial Intelligence Research*, 37:247–277.

Alec Radford, Jong Wook Kim, Chris Hallacy, Aditya Ramesh, Gabriel Goh, Sandhini Agarwal, Girish Sastry, Amanda Askell, Pamela Mishkin, Jack Clark, et al. 2021. Learning transferable visual models from natural language supervision. In *ICML*.

Mohammad Sadegh Rasooli, Chris Callison-Burch, and Derry Tanti Wijaya. 2021. "wikily" supervised neural translation tailored to cross-lingual tasks. In *EMNLP*.

Deb K Roy and Alex P Pentland. 2002. Learning words from sights and sounds: A computational model. *Cognitive science*, 26(1):113–146.

Shane Settle, Kartik Audhkhasi, Karen Livescu, and Michael Picheny. 2019. Acoustically grounded word embeddings for improved acoustics-to-word speech recognition. In *ICASSP*.

Lanbo She and Joyce Chai. 2016. Incremental acquisition of verb hypothesis space towards physical world interaction. In *ACL*.

Lanbo She and Joyce Chai. 2017. Interactive learning of grounded verb semantics towards human-robot communication. In *ACL*.

Freda Shi, Mirac Suzgun, Markus Freitag, Xuezhi Wang, Suraj Srivats, Soroush Vosoughi, Hyung Won Chung, Yi Tay, Sebastian Ruder, Denny Zhou, Dipanjan Das, and Jason Wei. 2023. Language models are multilingual chain-of-thought reasoners. In *ICLR*.

Haoyue Shi, Jiayuan Mao, Kevin Gimpel, and Karen Livescu. 2019. Visually grounded neural syntax acquisition. In *ACL*.

Haoyue Freda Shi. 2024. *Learning Language Structures through Grounding*. Ph.D. thesis, Toyota Technological Institute at Chicago.

Jeffrey Mark Siskind. 1996. A computational study of cross-situational techniques for learning word-to-meaning mappings. *Cognition*, 61(1-2):39–91.

Mark Steedman. 2000. *The Syntactic Process*. Cambridge, MA: MIT Press.

Luc Steels. 2003. Evolving grounded communication for robots. *Trends in cognitive sciences*, 7(7):308–312.

Luc Steels, Frédéric Kaplan, Angus Mcintyre, and Joris Van Looveren. 2000. Crucial factors in the origins of word meaning. In *In: Proceedings of the 3rd Conference on the Evolution of Language*.

Ruisi Su, Shruti Rijhwani, Hao Zhu, Junxian He, Xinyu Wang, Yonatan Bisk, and Graham Neubig. 2021. Dependency induction through the lens of visual perception. In *CoNLL*.

Alane Suhr, Mike Lewis, James Yeh, and Yoav Artzi. 2017. A corpus of natural language for visual reasoning. In *ACL*.

Hao Tan and Mohit Bansal. 2019. Lxmert: Learning cross-modality encoder representations from transformers. In *EMNLP-IJCNLP*.

Hao Tan and Mohit Bansal. 2020. Vokenization: Improving language understanding with contextualized, visual-grounded supervision. In *EMNLP*.

Lucien Tesnière. 1959. *Éléments de Syntaxe Structurale*. Librairie C. Klincksieck, Paris.

Chau Tran, Yuqing Tang, Xian Li, and Jiatao Gu. 2020. Cross-lingual retrieval for iterative self-supervised training. In *NeurIPS*.

Sida I. Wang, Percy Liang, and Christopher D. Manning. 2016. Learning language games through interaction. In *ACL*.

Fei Xu and Joshua B Tenenbaum. 2007. Word learning as bayesian inference. *Psychological review*, 114(2):245.

Lili Yu, Howard Chen, Sida I. Wang, Tao Lei, and Yoav Artzi. 2020. Interactive classification by asking informative questions. In *ACL*.

Songyang Zhang, Linfeng Song, Lifeng Jin, Kun Xu, Dong Yu, and Jiebo Luo. 2021. Video-aided unsupervised grammar induction. In *NAACL-HLT*.

Yanpeng Zhao and Ivan Titov. 2020. Visually grounded compound PCFGs. In *EMNLP*.

Hao Zhu, Yonatan Bisk, and Graham Neubig. 2022. Language learning from communicative goals and linguistic input. In *CogSci*.

LLMs and Copyright Risks: Benchmarks and Mitigation Approaches

Denghui Zhang
Stevens Institute of Technology
dzhang42@stevens.edu

Zhaozhuo Xu
Stevens Institute of Technology
zxu79@stevens.edu

Weijie Zhao
Rochester Institute of Technology
wjz@cs.rit.edu

Abstract

Large Language Models (LLMs) have revolutionized natural language processing, but their widespread use has raised significant copyright concerns. This tutorial addresses the complex intersection of LLMs and copyright law, providing researchers and practitioners with essential knowledge and tools to navigate this challenging landscape. The tutorial begins with an overview of relevant copyright principles and their application to AI, followed by an examination of specific copyright issues in LLM development and deployment. A key focus will be on technical approaches to copyright risk assessment and mitigation in LLMs. We will introduce benchmarks for evaluating copyright-related risks, including memorization detection and probing techniques. The tutorial will then cover practical mitigation strategies, such as machine unlearning, efficient fine-tuning methods, and alignment approaches to reduce copyright infringement risks. Ethical considerations and future directions in copyright-aware AI development will also be discussed.

1 Introduction

The landscape of artificial intelligence has been dramatically transformed by the advent of Large Language Models (LLMs) such as GPT and its successors (Lewis et al., 2019; Brown et al., 2020a; OpenAI, 2023; Zhang et al., 2022; Touvron et al., 2023). These powerful systems have not only revolutionized natural language processing but have also permeated diverse sectors including healthcare (Peng et al., 2023; Haupt and Marks, 2023), software development (Chen et al., 2021), finance (Yang et al., 2023; Wang et al., 2023b), and education (Firat, 2023; Fuchs, 2023). While LLMs have unlocked unprecedented capabilities in text generation and analysis, they have simultaneously given rise to complex legal and ethical challenges, particularly in the realm of copyright law. The ability of these models to produce human-like text has blurred the boundaries between original creation and potential copyright infringement, as evidenced by recent New York Times legal actions against AI company (nyt, 2023). This tutorial aims to navigate this intricate terrain, providing a comprehensive exploration of the copyright issues surrounding LLMs and equipping participants with the knowledge and tools to address these challenges.

In this tutorial, we will comprehensively review existing paradigms for copyright risk assessment and mitigation in LLMs, focusing on their contributions to responsible AI development and deployment. We categorize the approaches into probing and benchmarking, influence analysis, unlearning techniques, and finetuning-based behavior regulation. For probing and benchmarking, we will explore methodologies for creating quantitative measures to assess the extent of copyrighted content reproduction in LLM outputs. Influence analysis will cover the application of influence functions to detect and quantify the impact of potentially copyrighted material in training data. We will then examine machine unlearning techniques as a means to selectively remove knowledge of copyrighted content from trained LLMs. Finally, we will present efficient finetuning and alignment methodologies designed to modify LLM behavior with respect to copyright considerations. Participants will learn about recent trends and emerging challenges in copyright-aware LLM research, as well as resources and tools to implement these techniques. The tutorial aims to prompt thorough discussions regarding the impact of copyright considerations on LLM development and the broader implications for AI ethics and governance.

2 Tutorial Outline

We will cover four topics on how to measure and mitigate copyright risks of LLMs. **(1) LLMs Copyright Risks Probing and Benchmarking:** We will introduce and analyze state-of-the-art techniques

Proceedings of the 2025 Annual Conference of the Nations of the Americas Chapter of the Association for Computational Linguistics: Human Language Technologies: Tutorial Abstracts, pages 44–50

for probing LLMs to identify potential copyright infringements. This section will cover methodologies for creating benchmarks that quantitatively assess the extent of copyrighted content reproduction in LLM outputs. **(2) Influence Function for Copyright Detection in Training Data:** We will examine the application of influence functions, a technique from robust statistics, to detect and quantify the impact of potentially copyrighted material in LLM training datasets to model generations. This approach offers a principled way to trace model outputs back to specific training instances. **(3) Mitigating Copyright Risks via Machine Unlearning:** This section will discuss cutting-edge machine unlearning techniques as a means to selectively remove knowledge of copyrighted content from trained LLMs. We will discuss the theoretical foundations of unlearning algorithms and their practical implementation in the context of large-scale language models. **(4) Efficient Finetuning and Alignment to Regulate LLMs Behavior:** We will review efficient finetuning methodologies and alignment techniques designed to modify LLM behavior with respect to copyright considerations. This includes exploring parameter-efficient tuning methods and reinforcement learning approaches for aligning model outputs with copyright regulations.

3 Specification of the Tutorial

3.1 History

This tutorial has not been presented elsewhere. The presented topic has not been covered by previous AAAI/IJCAI/NeurIPS/ACL/EMNLP/NAACL tutorials in the past five years. The most related tutorial is the AAAI 2024 tutorial "Beyond Human Creativity: A Tutorial on Advancements in AI Generated Content" that covers the foundations, recent advancements, applications, and societal implications of large language models and diffusion models in text, image, video, and 3D object generation. They lack in-depth coverage on measuring and mitigating the potential risks of AI-generated content, which this tutorial aims to address.

3.2 Audience

Based on the level of interest in this topic, we expect around 50-100 participants from machine learning (ML) communities, data mining (DM) communities and natural language processing (NLP) communities.

3.3 Prerequisite Knowledge

While no specific background knowledge is assumed of the audience, it would be beneficial for attendees to have familiarity with basic machine learning and deep learning technologies, as well as pre-trained language models (e.g., BERT (Devlin et al., 2018), GPT (Brown et al., 2020b)) and generative AI concepts.

The following reading list could help provide background knowledge to the audience before attending this tutorial:

- Jialiang Xu, Shenglan Li, Zhaozhuo Xu, and Denghui Zhang. Do LLMs Know to Respect Copyright Notice? In EMNLP, 2024.
- Boyi Wei et al. Evaluating Copyright Takedown Methods for Language Models. In NeurIPS, 2024.
- Tong Chen, Akari Asai, et al. CopyBench: Measuring Literal and Non-Literal Reproduction of Copyright-Protected Text in Language Model Generation. In EMNLP, 2024.
- Yuanshun Yao, Xiaojun Xu, and Yang Liu. Large Language Model Unlearning. In ICLR, 2024
- Ronen Eldan and Mark Russinovich. Who's Harry Potter? Approximate Unlearning in LLMs. arXiv preprint arXiv:2310.02238, 2023.
- Huawei Lin, Jikai Long, Zhaozhuo Xu, and Weijie Zhao. Token-Wise Influential Training Data Retrieval for Large Language Models. In ACL, 2024.
- Wentao Guo, Jikai Long, Yimeng Zeng, Zirui Liu, Xinyu Yang, Yide Ran, Jacob R. Gardner, Osbert Bastani, Christopher De Sa, Xiaodong Yu, et al. Zeroth-Order Fine-Tuning of LLMs with Extreme Sparsity. In ICML, 2024.

4 Tutorial Content

4.1 LLMs Copyright Risks Probing and Benchmarking [50mins]

We will first discuss the concept of copyright infringement in the context of LLMs, highlighting how it differs across regions such as the U.S. and Europe. Then we review quantitative assessment methodologies for copyright infringement risks in LLMs. Research indicates that model memorization is a primary cause of potential infringement behavior (Carlini et al., 2021; Nasr et al., 2023; Karamolegkou et al., 2023). We will present the "memory profile" tool for statistical causal analysis of LLM memorization (Lesci et al., 2024) to factors like data positions in training steps. The CopyBench framework (Chen et al., 2024) will be presented as a means to quantify literal and non-literal overlap between LLM outputs and copyrighted material. Additionally, we present our recent work for evaluating LLM compliance with copyright restrictions on user-provided content and unauthorized commands (Xu et al., 2024). Through these methodologies, we aim to provide a multi-perspective approach and tutorial to assessing copyright risks in LLMs. This part is estimated to be 45 minutes, with 5 minutes for Q&A.

4.2 Influence Function for Copyright Detection in Training Data [50mins]

We will explore how to identify which training data contributed to a specific generation from a Large Language Model (LLM) using the proposed framework, RapidIn (Lin et al., 2024). For instance, when a generation is found to violate copyright, tracing it back to the most influential training data enables developers to filter out infringing data and retrain the model (Ladhak et al., 2023). Additionally, understanding the influence of training data on a specific generation is critical for tasks like machine unlearning (Yao et al., 2023a; Yu et al., 2023), improving explainability (Zhao et al., 2023), detoxification (Welbl et al., 2021; Dale et al., 2021), data cleansing and combating data poisoning (Yan et al., 2023; Wang et al., 2023a; Huang et al., 2023; Ladhak et al., 2023), as well as preserving privacy and security (Brown et al., 2022; Kandpal et al., 2022). RapidIn estimates the influence of training data by compressing gradient vectors over 200,000x, enabling efficient caching and retrieval, offering a practical solution for handling LLMs at scale and enabling crucial tasks like model retraining and machine unlearning. This part will be $\sim$45 minutes, with 5 minutes for Q&A.

4.3 Mitigating Copyright Risks via Machine Unlearning [50mins]

In this part, we will first review the recent research of applying LLM machine unlearning techniques to address copyright infringement issues. Specifically, Yao et al. (2023b) used a gradient ascent-based approach to unlearn copyrighted contents, while Eldan and Russinovich (2023) explored a similar method to unlearn the Harry Potter series. However, Shostack (2024) pointed out that remnants of the Harry Potter books remained in the modified model. More recently, Chen and Yang (2023) proposed adding unlearning layers in transformer blocks for sequential data forgetting, but this approach was only tested on a smaller model focused on movie reviews in a simulated setting. In contrast, our recent work (Dou et al., 2024) formally studies the copyright unlearning problem under the sequential/continual setting, and tries to address the trade-offs between unlearning efficacy and general knowledge retention based on weight saliency. This part will be around 45 minutes, with 5 minutes for Q&A.

4.4 Efficient Finetuning and Alignment to Regulate LLMs Behavior [50mins]

We propose to regulate the LLMs' behavior with memory-efficient fine-tuning strategies. We will introduce a memory-efficient LLM fine-tuning approach, denoted as Winner-Take-All Column-Row Sampling (WTA-CRS) (Liu et al., 2024), which outperforms the existing Low-Rank Adaptation (LoRA) (Hu et al., 2021) techniques with better memory savings. WTA-CRS reduces the memory required for storing activations during training by selectively sampling matrix elements, enabling larger batch sizes and reducing hardware constraints with minimal accuracy loss. Moreover, we will introduce a series of sparse zeroth-order optimization strategies (Guo et al., 2024) that perform backpropagation-free LLM fine-tuning by perturbing 0.1% of LLM parameters. These techniques are particularly effective in aligning LLM behavior to specific tasks, including compliance with copyright regulations, without incurring excessive computational overhead. By leveraging these innovative techniques, we aim to provide a scalable and practical approach to finetuning LLMs, ensuring they align with desired behavioral outcomes while also addressing resource constraints common in large-scale model deployment. This part will be around 45 minutes, with 5 minutes for Q&A.

4.5 Conclusion and Remaining Challenges [30mins]

We will conclude the tutorial by summarizing the key concepts discussed, including techniques for mitigating copyright risks in LLMs. While progress has been made, several challenges remain: (1) Scaling Up Infringement Detection: Existing methods for detecting potential copyright violations struggle to scale when applied to large databases of copyrighted works. Developing more efficient and scalable approaches remains a critical challenge for the future. (2) Internal Concept Decomposition of Copyright Behavior: A deeper understanding of how LLMs internalize and represent copyrighted material is needed. Current methods focus on literal output analysis, but advances in decomposing internal representations could lead to more effective unlearning techniques and better regulation of model behavior.

These open challenges underscore the need for ongoing research to ensure the responsible use of LLMs while balancing innovation and copyright compliance.

5 Tutorial Presenters

Denghui Zhang is An assistant Professor in the School of Business at Stevens Institute of Technology. He studies the interplay between LLMs/GenAI, legal and socioethical issue, business and innovation. His work is published in refereed venues, such as IEEE TKDE, SIGKDD, EMNLP, AAAI, etc., and won Best Student Paper award at 2023 International Conference on Information Systems.

Zhaozhuo Xu is an Assistant Professor at Stevens Institute of Technology, focusing on scalable and sustainable ML. His work, published in venues like NeurIPS, ICML, and ICLR, has been adopted by Huggingface and startups. He is the organizer of Research On Algorithms & Data Structures (ROADS) to Mega-AI Models Workshop at MLSys 2023.

Weijie Zhao is an Assistant Professor in the department of computer science at RIT. He is investigating a broad collection of exciting problems in big data, machine learning systems, AI security, scientific data processing, and database systems.

David Atkinson, J.D., is a lecturer at the McCombs School of Business at The University of Texas at Austin, where he teaches courses on law, ethics, artificial intelligence, and the legal environment of business. He also serves as legal counsel for the Allen Institute for Artificial Intelligence, specializing in privacy, security, export control, and contracts. Previously, he was senior corporate counsel at the autonomous trucking company TuSimple and a technology scout for the U.S. Army. Additionally, Atkinson has served as legal counsel for the education technology company PowerSchool, worked as an InSITE consultant fellow for startups, and co-founded the legal education company Illustrated Law. He also holds master's degrees from Harvard and Kansas State University and a B.S. from Truman State University.

Boyi Wei is a Ph.D. student at Princeton University, advised by Peter Henderson. His research focuses on aligning machine learning systems, especially on understanding the safety alignment of language models and exploring related legal and policy issues. He received his B.Sc from University of Science and Technology of China.

Xiusi Chen is a Postdoctoral Research Fellow at the University of Illinois Urbana-Champaign, working with Prof. Heng Ji. He received his Ph.D. in Computer Science at the University of California, Los Angeles, advised by Prof. Wei Wang. Xiusi's research focuses on enhancing LLM reasoning, alignment, and decision-making. Xiusi has been awarded the SDM Best Poster Award Honorable Mention. His research has generated over 40 publications in top-tier venues in the fields of data mining, natural language processing, machine learning and information retrieval. Xiusi has been invited as a reviewer or a program committee member for conferences including KDD, ICML, NeurIPS, ICLR, ACL Rolling Review, etc.

Qingyun Wang is the incoming assistant professor at William & Mary. He is among the first researchers to develop a virtual scientific research assistant for literature-based discovery by extracting and synthesizing insights from papers. He received the NAACL-HLT 2021 Best Demo Reward. He has experience presenting tutorials at EMNLP 2021, EACL 2024, and LREC-COLING 2024. He organized AI4Research workshop at AAAI 2025 and the Language + Molecules Workshop at ACL 2024.

Jing Gao is an Associate Professor at Purdue University's Elmore Family School of Electrical and Computer Engineering. Her research spans data mining, focusing on information veracity, crowdsourcing, knowledge graphs, anomaly detection, and multi-source data integration, with applications in healthcare, cybersecurity, and education. She has received the NSF CAREER Award, ICDM Tao Li Award, and SDM/IBM Early Career Data Mining Researcher Award. She also serves as an editor for ACM Transactions on Intelligent Systems and Technology and IEEE Transactions on Knowledge and Data Engineering.

Diversity considerations

In this tutorial, we prioritize diversity considerations across multiple dimensions. We will incorporate the use of multilingual data to demonstrate how the described methods for copyright risk assessment and mitigation scale effectively across various languages and domains, highlighting the global relevance of these challenges. The instructional team will include both senior and junior researchers to ensure a range of perspectives and expertise, promoting an inclusive learning environment. Additionally, we emphasize demographic and geographical diversity among instructors to reflect the international nature of AI ethics and copyright issues. To further encourage diverse audience participation, we plan to actively engage underrepresented groups through targeted outreach efforts and provide accessible resources for participants from varying backgrounds and regions. This approach aims to foster a richer, more inclusive dialogue on the ethical considerations of LLMs.

Ethics Statement

The responsible development and deployment of Large Language Models (LLMs) necessitates a careful balance between innovation and ethical considerations, particularly in the context of copyright law. This tutorial acknowledges the profound implications that LLMs have on intellectual property and emphasizes the importance of addressing these challenges proactively.

We are committed to advancing the understanding of LLMs while ensuring that their capabilities are used ethically and in accordance with legal frameworks. Through this tutorial, we aim to foster transparency in AI systems, promote the use of copyright-aware methodologies, and advocate for responsible AI practices. We encourage participants to engage in thoughtful discussions regarding the broader societal impact of LLMs, especially in terms of fairness, accountability, and respect for the rights of content creators.

By equipping attendees with tools for assessing and mitigating copyright risks, we hope to contribute to the development of AI systems that are not only powerful but also aligned with ethical principles and legal norms.

References

2023. New york times company v. microsoft corporation and openai, inc. Filed Dec. 27, 2023.

Hannah Brown, Katherine Lee, Fatemehsadat Mireshghallah, Reza Shokri, and Florian Tramèr. 2022. What does it mean for a language model to preserve privacy? In *FAccT '22: 2022 ACM Conference on Fairness, Accountability, and Transparency*, pages 2280–2292, Seoul, Republic of Korea.

Tom Brown, Benjamin Mann, Nick Ryder, Melanie Subbiah, Jared D Kaplan, Prafulla Dhariwal, Arvind Neelakantan, Pranav Shyam, Girish Sastry, Amanda Askell, et al. 2020a. Language models are few-shot learners. *Advances in neural information processing systems*, 33:1877–1901.

Tom Brown, Benjamin Mann, Nick Ryder, Melanie Subbiah, Jared D Kaplan, Prafulla Dhariwal, Arvind Neelakantan, Pranav Shyam, Girish Sastry, Amanda Askell, et al. 2020b. Language models are few-shot learners. *Advances in neural information processing systems*, 33:1877–1901.

Nicholas Carlini, Florian Tramer, Eric Wallace, Matthew Jagielski, Ariel Herbert-Voss, Katherine Lee, Adam Roberts, Tom Brown, Dawn Song, Ulfar Erlingsson, et al. 2021. Extracting training data from large language models. In *30th USENIX Security Symposium (USENIX Security 21)*, pages 2633–2650.

Jiaao Chen and Diyi Yang. 2023. Unlearn what you want to forget: Efficient unlearning for llms. *arXiv preprint arXiv:2310.20150*.

Mark Chen, Jerry Tworek, Heewoo Jun, Qiming Yuan, Henrique Ponde de Oliveira Pinto, Jared Kaplan, Harri Edwards, Yuri Burda, Nicholas Joseph, Greg Brockman, et al. 2021. Evaluating large language models trained on code. *arXiv preprint arXiv:2107.03374*.

Tong Chen, Akari Asai, Niloofar Mireshghallah, Sewon Min, James Grimmelmann, Yejin Choi, Hannaneh Hajishirzi, Luke Zettlemoyer, and Pang Wei Koh. 2024. Copybench: Measuring literal and non-literal reproduction of copyright-protected text in language model generation. *ArXiv preprint*, abs/2407.07087.

David Dale, Anton Voronov, Daryna Dementieva, Varvara Logacheva, Olga Kozlova, Nikita Semenov, and Alexander Panchenko. 2021. Text detoxification using large pre-trained neural models. In *Proceedings of the 2021 Conference on Empirical Methods in Natural Language Processing, EMNLP*, pages 7979–7996, Virtual Event / Punta Cana, Dominican Republic.

Jacob Devlin, Ming-Wei Chang, Kenton Lee, and Kristina Toutanova. 2018. Bert: Pre-training of deep bidirectional transformers for language understanding. *arXiv preprint arXiv:1810.04805*.

Guangyao Dou, Zheyuan Liu, Qing Lyu, Kaize Ding, and Eric Wong. 2024. Avoiding copyright infringement via machine unlearning. *arXiv preprint arXiv:2406.10952*.

Ronen Eldan and Mark Russinovich. 2023. Who's harry potter? approximate unlearning in llms. *arXiv preprint arXiv:2310.02238*.

Mehmet Firat. 2023. How chat gpt can transform autodidactic experiences and open education?

Kevin Fuchs. 2023. Exploring the opportunities and challenges of nlp models in higher education: is chat gpt a blessing or a curse? In *Frontiers in Education*, volume 8, page 1166682. Frontiers Media SA.

Wentao Guo, Jikai Long, Yimeng Zeng, Zirui Liu, Xinyu Yang, Yide Ran, Jacob R Gardner, Osbert Bastani, Christopher De Sa, Xiaodong Yu, et al. 2024. Zeroth-order fine-tuning of llms with extreme sparsity. *arXiv preprint arXiv:2406.02913*.

Claudia E Haupt and Mason Marks. 2023. Ai-generated medical advice—gpt and beyond. *Jama*, 329(16):1349–1350.

Edward J Hu, Yelong Shen, Phillip Wallis, Zeyuan Allen-Zhu, Yuanzhi Li, Shean Wang, Lu Wang, and Weizhu Chen. 2021. Lora: Low-rank adaptation of large language models. *arXiv preprint arXiv:2106.09685*.

Hai Huang, Zhengyu Zhao, Michael Backes, Yun Shen, and Yang Zhang. 2023. Composite backdoor attacks against large language models. *CoRR*, abs/2310.07676.

Nikhil Kandpal, Eric Wallace, and Colin Raffel. 2022. Deduplicating training data mitigates privacy risks in language models. In *International Conference on Machine Learning, ICML*, volume 162 of *Proceedings of Machine Learning Research*, pages 10697–10707, Baltimore, Maryland.

Antonia Karamolegkou, Jiaang Li, Li Zhou, and Anders Søgaard. 2023. Copyright violations and large language models. *ArXiv preprint*, abs/2310.13771.

Faisal Ladhak, Esin Durmus, and Tatsunori Hashimoto. 2023. Contrastive error attribution for finetuned language models. In *Proceedings of the 61st Annual Meeting of the Association for Computational Linguistics (Volume 1: Long Papers), ACL*, pages 11482–11498, Toronto, Canada.

Pietro Lesci, Clara Meister, Thomas Hofmann, Andreas Vlachos, and Tiago Pimentel. 2024. Causal estimation of memorisation profiles. In *Proceedings of the 62nd Annual Meeting of the Association for Computational Linguistics (Volume 1: Long Papers)*, pages 15616–15635. Association for Computational Linguistics.

Mike Lewis, Yinhan Liu, Naman Goyal, Marjan Ghazvininejad, Abdelrahman Mohamed, Omer Levy, Ves Stoyanov, and Luke Zettlemoyer. 2019. Bart: Denoising sequence-to-sequence pre-training for natural language generation, translation, and comprehension. *arXiv preprint arXiv:1910.13461*.

Huawei Lin, Jikai Long, Zhaozhuo Xu, and Weijie Zhao. 2024. Token-wise influential training data retrieval for large language models. In *Proceedings of the 62nd Annual Meeting of the Association for Computational Linguistics (Volume 1: Long Papers), ACL 2024, Bangkok, Thailand, August 11-16, 2024*, pages 841–860. Association for Computational Linguistics.

Zirui Liu, Guanchu Wang, Shaochen Henry Zhong, Zhaozhuo Xu, Daochen Zha, Ruixiang Ryan Tang, Zhimeng Stephen Jiang, Kaixiong Zhou, Vipin Chaudhary, Shuai Xu, et al. 2024. Winner-take-all column row sampling for memory efficient adaptation of language model. *Advances in Neural Information Processing Systems*, 36.

Milad Nasr, N Carlini, J Hayase, M Jagielski, AF Cooper, D Ippolito, CA Choquette-Choo, E Wallace, F Tramer, and K Lee. 2023. Scalable extraction of training data from (production) language models (2023). *ArXiv preprint*, abs/2311.17035.

OpenAI. 2023. Gpt-4 technical report. In *arXiv*.

Cheng Peng, Xi Yang, Aokun Chen, Kaleb E Smith, Nima PourNejatian, Anthony B Costa, Cheryl Martin, Mona G Flores, Ying Zhang, Tanja Magoc, et al. 2023. A study of generative large language model for medical research and healthcare. *NPJ digital medicine*, 6(1):210.

Adam Shostack. 2024. The boy who survived: Removing harry potter from an llm is harder than reported. *arXiv preprint arXiv:2403.12082*.

Hugo Touvron, Thibaut Lavril, Gautier Izacard, Xavier Martinet, Marie-Anne Lachaux, Timothée Lacroix, Baptiste Rozière, Naman Goyal, Eric Hambro, Faisal Azhar, et al. 2023. Llama: Open and efficient foundation language models. *arXiv preprint arXiv:2302.13971*.

Jiongxiao Wang, Zichen Liu, Keun Hee Park, Muhao Chen, and Chaowei Xiao. 2023a. Adversarial demonstration attacks on large language models. *CoRR*, abs/2305.14950.

Neng Wang, Hongyang Yang, and Christina Dan Wang. 2023b. Fingpt: Instruction tuning benchmark for open-source large language models in financial datasets. *NeurIPS Workshop on Instruction Tuning and Instruction Following*.

Johannes Welbl, Amelia Glaese, Jonathan Uesato, Sumanth Dathathri, John Mellor, Lisa Anne Hendricks, Kirsty Anderson, Pushmeet Kohli, Ben Coppin, and Po-Sen Huang. 2021. Challenges in detoxifying language models. In *Findings of the Association for Computational Linguistics: EMNLP*, pages

2447–2469, Virtual Event / Punta Cana, Dominican Republic.

Jialiang Xu, Shenglan Li, Zhaozhuo Xu, and Denghui Zhang. 2024. Do llms know to respect copyright notice? In *Proceedings of the 2024 Conference on Empirical Methods in Natural Language Processing*.

Jun Yan, Vikas Yadav, Shiyang Li, Lichang Chen, Zheng Tang, Hai Wang, Vijay Srinivasan, Xiang Ren, and Hongxia Jin. 2023. Backdooring instruction-tuned large language models with virtual prompt injection. In *NeurIPS 2023 Workshop on Backdoors in Deep Learning-The Good, the Bad, and the Ugly*.

Hongyang Yang, Xiao-Yang Liu, and Christina Dan Wang. 2023. Fingpt: Open-source financial large language models. *arXiv preprint arXiv:2306.06031*.

Yuanshun Yao, Xiaojun Xu, and Yang Liu. 2023a. Large language model unlearning. *CoRR*, abs/2310.10683.

Yuanshun Yao, Xiaojun Xu, and Yang Liu. 2023b. Large language model unlearning. *arXiv preprint arXiv:2310.10683*.

Charles Yu, Sullam Jeoung, Anish Kasi, Pengfei Yu, and Heng Ji. 2023. Unlearning bias in language models by partitioning gradients. In *Findings of the Association for Computational Linguistics: ACL*, pages 6032–6048, Toronto, Canada.

Susan Zhang, Stephen Roller, Naman Goyal, Mikel Artetxe, Moya Chen, Shuohui Chen, Christopher Dewan, Mona Diab, Xian Li, Xi Victoria Lin, et al. 2022. Opt: Open pre-trained transformer language models. *ArXiv preprint*, abs/2205.01068.

Haiyan Zhao, Hanjie Chen, Fan Yang, Ninghao Liu, Huiqi Deng, Hengyi Cai, Shuaiqiang Wang, Dawei Yin, and Mengnan Du. 2023. Explainability for large language models: A survey. *CoRR*, abs/2309.01029.

Social Intelligence in the Age of LLMs

Hao Zhu[*], **Bodhisattwa Prasad Majumder**[†], **Dirk Hovy**[◇], **Diyi Yang**[*]
[*]Stanford University [†]Allen Institute for AI [◇]Bocconi University

1 Motivation and Objectives

With the emergence of Large Language Models (LLMs), we now have unprecedented opportunities to incorporate human-like communication and context-aware interactions into artificial systems. But what is the current state of LLMs' capability of social interaction? Can they truly understand social scenarios, perform social reasoning, or interact with humans as socially competent agents? We propose this tutorial as an introduction to and an overview of different aspects of artificial social intelligence and their relationship with LLMs.

In this tutorial, we will explore these questions by introducing scientific methods for evaluating social intelligence in LLMs, highlighting the key challenges, and identifying promising research directions. Participants will not only gain a comprehensive overview of the field's progress, but also acquire technical skills on analysing and developing LLM-based social intelligence.

2 Tutorial Outline

This will be a **three-hour tutorial** devoted to the **cutting-edge topic** of *Social Intelligence and Large Language Models*, divided into four themes. Each theme will take 40 minutes including Q&A. We provide a sample tutorial schedule in Table 1 for a morning tutorial. Each theme includes an overview of the corresponding topics, and a deep dive into a set of representative studies. We will conclude our tutorial by highlighting challenges and research opportunities in the field.

Time	Event	Speaker
09:00-09:05	Opening	Hao Zhu
09:05-09:45	Theme 1	Diyi Yang
09:45-09:50	Break	-
09:50-10:30	Theme 2	Bodhisattwa Prasad Majumder
10:30-10:35	Break	-
10:35-11:15	Theme 3	Dirk Hovy
11:15-11:20	Break	-
11:20-12:00	Theme 4	Hao Zhu

Table 1: Proposed schedule of events.

Theme 1: LLM + Culture and Norm (40 mins)

Social communication takes place within a cultural context, and understanding the influence of culture is important for conflict resolution and decision-making. As LLMs being used to produce vast amounts of data, they reflect and potentially influence social norms and cultural narratives embedded with the data. In this part, we aim to provide a deep dive into how LLMs can facilitate cross-cultural exchange and understanding, as well as how they perpetuate stereotypes and shape societal norms negatively, as a main case study of examining social intelligence in LLMs. We will first share how existing research quantifies cultural awareness (Naous et al., 2023; Ryan et al., 2024) and social norms in and of large language models, and also provide an overview of different multilingual and multicultural evaluations (Bhutani et al., 2024; Myung et al., 2024) that the language technologies communities have worked on. In addition to measuring culture and norm in LLMs, we plan to discuss how to develop more culturally aware and socially aware language technologies by focusing on how one can design culturally grounded objectives (Zhou et al., 2023a), represent culturally relevant concepts and entities as knowledge base (Shi et al., 2024), transfer learning and how diverse cultural and norm preferences are leveraged to align LLMs with such diverse intelligence (Kirk et al., 2024).

Theme 2: Social Reasoning (40 mins)

Social reasoning builds upon the foundations of the theory of mind and beliefs about the world. As LLMs become increasingly anthropomorphized due to their ability to interact like humans, it is crucial to critically investigate their true capabilities. Researchers have been employing various NLP techniques to evaluate LLMs on social reasoning tasks, assessing their ability to infer and interpret observed and perceived beliefs about the social world. We will discuss an array of frame-

Proceedings of the 2025 Annual Conference of the Nations of the Americas Chapter of the Association for Computational Linguistics: Human Language Technologies: Tutorial Abstracts, pages 51–55

works and benchmarks that aim to evaluate LLM's ability to perform social reasoning. We will investigate methods that tend to improve LLM's intrinsic ability to reason in a social scenario and identify the research gaps that remain in achieving a level of anthropomorphism, tying them to the continuing development of cutting-edge NLP methods to handle diverse social contexts.

Theme 3: Social Demographics (40 mins)

Language is used by people to communicate with other people, and who says something is often as important as what is said (Lynn et al., 2017). Our sociodemographic identity shapes both how we are perceived and how we choose to express ourselves. The meaning of a sentence can change depending on both the speaker's and the listener's sociodemographic profile (Hovy and Yang, 2021). NLP models do so far rarely model sociodemographic aspects of speaker or listener, but there is increasingly research showing the importance of doing so (Hovy, 2015). We will discuss what sociodemographic factors influence language, and in what ways, and how those can be modeled (Lauscher et al., 2022; Soni et al., 2024). We will specifically talk about persona-based prompting in LLMs (Cheng et al., 2023), which allows us now to explicitly incorporate sociodemographics into a model – or does it?

Theme 4: LLM-based Social Agents (40 mins)

Humans' ability to achieve and balance complex, multifaceted social goals in our interactions with others is a crucial part of our social intelligence as a species (Kihlstrom and Cantor, 2000; Tomasello, 2019). In this theme, we will focus on the interactive aspect of social intelligence. We first introduce the various environments where we can ground the social agents in, including text-based simulation environments (Zhou et al., 2023b; Park et al., 2023), virtual environments (Liu et al., 2023), simulated embodied environments (Biswas et al., 2022; team, 2024; Guo et al., 2024), and physical environments (Wang et al., 2024a). We will then introduce various evaluation metrics for social agents in these environments, including qualitative metrics from user surveys, quantitative metrics based on the outcome of the social interaction, and model-based evaluation using large language models. The third part of this theme will introduce various method for improving social intelligence in LLM-based agents, including prompting and in-context learning, *e.g.* Ma et al. (2024), fine-tuning, *e.g.* Wan et al. (2023), and reinforcement learning, *e.g.* Wang et al. (2024b). Finally, we will highlight several applications of social agents, including education (Liu et al., 2024), health (Mukherjee et al., 2024), and policy (Mou et al., 2024), and potential risks of applying social agents in the real world (Matz et al., 2024; Kasirzadeh, 2024). For each of the four parts in this theme, we will deep dive into the 1 to 2 most representative papers, including the technical details, but also offer an overview of the latest progress.

3 Tutorial Presenters

Hao Zhu is a postdoctoral scholar in the Computer Science Department at Stanford University. He got a PhD from Carnegie Mellon University. He focuses on artificial social intelligence, and published relevant papers in various NLP, LLM, ML, CV, Robotics and CogSci conferences. Hao led the organization of the first workshop on theory of mind at ICML 2023.

Bodhisattwa Prasad Majumder Bodhisattwa Prasad Majumder is a Research Scientist at the Allen Institute for AI. One of his key research interests is the development of interactive and communicative agents for social and scientific reasoning. He received his Ph.D. from UC San Diego where he received the CSE Dissertation Award (2024). Bodhisattwa was a keynote speaker at the Word-Play workshop at ACL 2024 and a panelist at the Theory of Mind workshop at ICML 2024. He co-organized the workshop on representation learning and commonsense reasoning at ACL 2022. Bodhisattwa also co-authored a best-selling book on Practical Natural Language Processing that is published in 4 languages and internationally adapted across several universities and organizations.

Dirk Hovy is a Professor in the Computing Sciences Department of Bocconi University. He got a PhD from USC's Information Sciences Institute, and a master's degree in sociolinguistics from Marburg University in Germany. Dirk is interested in what computers can tell us about language, and what language can tell us about society. He has authored over 150 articles on these topics, including 3 best and one outstanding paper awards, and published two textbooks on NLP in Python for social scientists. Dirk has co-founded and organized several workshops (on computational social science, ethics, cultural aspects, and hate speech in NLP), and was a local organizer for the EMNLP 2017 conference. He leads an ERC Starting Grant project on sociodemographic bias in NLP models.

Diyi Yang is an assistant professor in the Computer Science Department at Stanford University. Her research focuses on human-centered natural language processing and computational social science. Diyi has organized four workshops at NLP conferences: Widening NLP Workshops at NAACL 2018 and ACL 2019, Casual Inference workshop at EMNLP 2021, NLG Evaluation workshop at EMNLP 2021, and Shared Stories and Lessons Learned workshop at EMNLP 2022. She also gave a tutorial at ACL 2022 on Learning with Limited Data, and a tutorial at EACL 2023 on Summarizing Conversations at Scale. Diyi and Sherry have co-developed a new course on Human-Centered NLP that has been offered at both Stanford and CMU.

4 Diversity Considerations

We will make our tutorial materials digitally accessible to all participants. During the tutorial sessions, we will work with student volunteers to encourage open dialogue and promote active listening, allowing participants to share their thoughts and experiences without fear of judgment. After the tutorial, we will actively collect feedback to identify areas for improvement related to diversity and inclusion and share it with future tutorial presenters.

Our presenter team will share our tutorial with a worldwide audience by promoting it on social media, and to diverse research communities. Our presenters include both junior and senior researchers. Thus, we have diversified instructors which will also help encourage diverse audience. Diyi has experience co-organizing Widening NLP Workshops at both NAACL and ACL, and actively works on inviting undergraduate students to research and promoting diversity such as by speaking at AI4ALL and local high-schools at Atlanta. We will work with ACL/NAACL D&I teams, and consult resources such as the BIG directory to diversify our audience participation.

5 Reading List and Prerequisite

The tutorial is targeted toward NLP researchers and practitioners working with humans.

Breadth While we will give pointers to dozens of relevant papers over the course of the tutorial, we plan to cover around 15 research papers in close detail. Only 4 of the "deep dive" papers will come from the presenter team.

1. Having beer after prayer? measuring cultural bias in large language models. (Naous et al., 2023)
2. Unintended impacts of llm alignment on global representation. (Ryan et al., 2024)
3. Seegull multilingual: a dataset of geo-culturally situated stereotypes. (Bhutani et al., 2024)
4. Cross-cultural transfer learning for Chinese offensive language detection. (Zhou et al., 2023a)
5. The prism alignment project: What participatory, representative and individualised human feedback reveals about the subjective and multicultural alignment of large language models. (Kirk et al., 2024)
6. Human centered NLP with user-factor adaptation. (Lynn et al., 2017)
7. Demographic factors improve classification performance. (Hovy, 2015)
8. SocioProbe: What, when, and where language models learn about sociodemographics. (Lauscher et al., 2022)
9. Comparing pretrained human language models: Is it better with human context as groups, individual traits, or both? (Soni et al., 2024)
10. Marked personas: Using natural language prompts to measure stereotypes in language models (Cheng et al., 2023)
11. Becoming human: A theory of ontogeny. (Tomasello, 2019)
12. SOTOPIA: Interactive Evaluation for Social Intelligence in Language Agents. (Zhou et al., 2023b)
13. Computational language acquisition with theory of mind. (Liu et al., 2023)
14. Mosaic: A modular system for assistive and interactive cooking. (Wang et al., 2024a)

6 Tutorial Details

Audience Size We expect the audience size to be around 100 for a physical conference, and around 150 for a virtual conference. Our tutorial will likely bring a similar audience as the NLP+HCI workshop (`https://sites.google.com/view/hciandnlp-2021/home?authuser=0`).

Open Access We will put the slides, code, and other teaching materials online for public access, as well as consent to adding the video recording of our tutorial in the ACL Anthology.

7 Sharing of Tutorial Material

We plan to make all teaching material available online and agree to allow the publication of slides and video recordings in the ACL anthology.

8 Pedagogical Material

We plan to do some short hands-on exercises to let the audience try to prompt LLMs for the social intelligence tasks introduced in this tutorial.

9 Ethics Statement

When AI is used in social scenarios, the biases and stereotypes might lead to undesirable consequences. The goal of this tutorial is to offer the audience the tools to evaluate these biases and stereotypes and to mitigate them. We would also introduce latest progress of understanding the risks and safety issues of applying LLMs in the real world.

References

Mukul Bhutani, Kevin Robinson, Vinodkumar Prabhakaran, Shachi Dave, and Sunipa Dev. 2024. Seegull multilingual: a dataset of geo-culturally situated stereotypes. *arXiv preprint arXiv:2403.05696*.

Abhijat Biswas, Allan Wang, Gustavo Silvera, Aaron Steinfeld, and Henny Admoni. 2022. Socnavbench: A grounded simulation testing framework for evaluating social navigation. *J. Hum.-Robot Interact.*

Myra Cheng, Esin Durmus, and Dan Jurafsky. 2023. Marked personas: Using natural language prompts to measure stereotypes in language models. In *Proceedings of the 61st Annual Meeting of the Association for Computational Linguistics (Volume 1: Long Papers)*, pages 1504–1532, Toronto, Canada. Association for Computational Linguistics.

Xudong Guo, Kaixuan Huang, Jiale Liu, Wenhui Fan, Natalia Vélez, Qingyun Wu, Huazheng Wang, Thomas L. Griffiths, and Mengdi Wang. 2024. Embodied llm agents learn to cooperate in organized teams.

Dirk Hovy. 2015. Demographic factors improve classification performance. In *Proceedings of the 53rd Annual Meeting of the Association for Computational Linguistics and the 7th International Joint Conference on Natural Language Processing (Volume 1: Long Papers)*, pages 752–762, Beijing, China. Association for Computational Linguistics.

Dirk Hovy and Diyi Yang. 2021. The importance of modeling social factors of language: Theory and practice. In *Proceedings of the 2021 Conference of the North American Chapter of the Association for Computational Linguistics: Human Language Technologies*, pages 588–602, Online. Association for Computational Linguistics.

Atoosa Kasirzadeh. 2024. Two types of ai existential risk: Decisive and accumulative.

John F Kihlstrom and Nancy Cantor. 2000. Social intelligence. *Handbook of intelligence*, 2:359–379.

Hannah Rose Kirk, Alexander Whitefield, Paul Röttger, Andrew Bean, Katerina Margatina, Juan Ciro, Rafael Mosquera, Max Bartolo, Adina Williams, He He, et al. 2024. The prism alignment project: What participatory, representative and individualised human feedback reveals about the subjective and multicultural alignment of large language models. *arXiv preprint arXiv:2404.16019*.

Anne Lauscher, Federico Bianchi, Samuel R. Bowman, and Dirk Hovy. 2022. SocioProbe: What, when, and where language models learn about sociodemographics. In *Proceedings of the 2022 Conference on Empirical Methods in Natural Language Processing*, pages 7901–7918, Abu Dhabi, United Arab Emirates. Association for Computational Linguistics.

Andy Liu, Hao Zhu, Emmy Liu, Yonatan Bisk, and Graham Neubig. 2023. Computational language acquisition with theory of mind. In *The Eleventh International Conference on Learning Representations*.

Jiawen Liu, Yuanyuan Yao, Pengcheng An, and Qi Wang. 2024. Peergpt: Probing the roles of llm-based peer agents as team moderators and participants in children's collaborative learning. In *Extended Abstracts of the 2024 CHI Conference on Human Factors in Computing Systems*, CHI EA '24, New York, NY, USA. Association for Computing Machinery.

Veronica Lynn, Youngseo Son, Vivek Kulkarni, Niranjan Balasubramanian, and H. Andrew Schwartz. 2017. Human centered NLP with user-factor adaptation. In *Proceedings of the 2017 Conference on Empirical Methods in Natural Language Processing*, pages 1146–1155, Copenhagen, Denmark. Association for Computational Linguistics.

Qianou Ma, Hua Shen, Kenneth Koedinger, and Tongshuang Wu. 2024. How to teach programming in the AI era? using LLMs as a teachable agent for debugging. In *International Conference on Artificial Intelligence in Education*.

SC Matz, JD Teeny, Sumer S Vaid, H Peters, GM Harari, and M Cerf. 2024. The potential of generative ai for personalized persuasion at scale. *Scientific Reports*, 14(1):4692.

Xinyi Mou, Zhongyu Wei, and Xuanjing Huang. 2024. Unveiling the truth and facilitating change: Towards agent-based large-scale social movement simulation.

Subhabrata Mukherjee, Paul Gamble, Markel Sanz Ausin, Neel Kant, Kriti Aggarwal, Neha Manjunath, Debajyoti Datta, Zhengliang Liu, Jiayuan Ding, Sophia Busacca, Cezanne Bianco, Swapnil Sharma, Rae Lasko, Michelle Voisard, Sanchay Harneja, Darya Filippova, Gerry Meixiong, Kevin Cha, Amir Youssefi, Meyhaa Buvanesh, Howard Weingram, Sebastian Bierman-Lytle, Harpreet Singh Mangat, Kim Parikh, Saad Godil, and Alex Miller. 2024. Polaris: A safety-focused llm constellation architecture for healthcare.

Junho Myung, Nayeon Lee, Yi Zhou, Jiho Jin, Rifki Afina Putri, Dimosthenis Antypas, Hsuvas Borkakoty, Eunsu Kim, Carla Perez-Almendros, Abinew Ali Ayele, et al. 2024. Blend: A benchmark for llms on everyday knowledge in diverse cultures and languages. *arXiv preprint arXiv:2406.09948*.

Tarek Naous, Michael J Ryan, Alan Ritter, and Wei Xu. 2023. Having beer after prayer? measuring cultural bias in large language models. *arXiv preprint arXiv:2305.14456*.

Joon Sung Park, Joseph O'Brien, Carrie Jun Cai, Meredith Ringel Morris, Percy Liang, and Michael S Bernstein. 2023. Generative agents: Interactive simulacra of human behavior. In *Proceedings of the 36th annual acm symposium on user interface software and technology*, pages 1–22.

Michael J Ryan, William Held, and Diyi Yang. 2024. Unintended impacts of llm alignment on global representation. *arXiv preprint arXiv:2402.15018*.

Weiyan Shi, Ryan Li, Yutong Zhang, Caleb Ziems, Raya Horesh, Rogério Abreu de Paula, Diyi Yang, et al. 2024. Culturebank: An online community-driven knowledge base towards culturally aware language technologies. *arXiv preprint arXiv:2404.15238*.

Nikita Soni, Niranjan Balasubramanian, H. Andrew Schwartz, and Dirk Hovy. 2024. Comparing pretrained human language models: Is it better with human context as groups, individual traits, or both? In *Proceedings of the 14th Workshop on Computational Approaches to Subjectivity, Sentiment, & Social Media Analysis*, pages 316–328, Bangkok, Thailand. Association for Computational Linguistics.

OpenGenerativeAI team. 2024. Evaluate llms in real time with street fighter iii.

Michael Tomasello. 2019. *Becoming human: A theory of ontogeny*. Harvard University Press.

Yanming Wan, Jiayuan Mao, and Joshua B. Tenenbaum. 2023. Handmethat: Human-robot communication in physical and social environments.

Huaxiaoyue Wang, Kushal Kedia, Juntao Ren, Rahma Abdullah, Atiksh Bhardwaj, Angela Chao, Kelly Y Chen, Nathaniel Chin, Prithwish Dan, Xinyi Fan, et al. 2024a. Mosaic: A modular system for assistive and interactive cooking. In *2nd Workshop on Mobile Manipulation and Embodied Intelligence at ICRA 2024*.

Ruiyi Wang, Haofei Yu, Wenxin Zhang, Zhengyang Qi, Maarten Sap, Graham Neubig, Yonatan Bisk, and Hao Zhu. 2024b. Sotopia-π: Interactive learning of socially intelligent language agents.

Li Zhou, Laura Cabello, Yong Cao, and Daniel Hershcovich. 2023a. Cross-cultural transfer learning for Chinese offensive language detection. In *Proceedings of the First Workshop on Cross-Cultural Considerations in NLP (C3NLP)*, pages 8–15, Dubrovnik, Croatia. Association for Computational Linguistics.

Xuhui Zhou, Hao Zhu, Leena Mathur, Ruohong Zhang, Haofei Yu, Zhengyang Qi, Louis-Philippe Morency, Yonatan Bisk, Daniel Fried, Graham Neubig, and Maarten Sap. 2023b. SOTOPIA: Interactive Evaluation for Social Intelligence in Language Agents.

Association for Computational Linguistics
209 N. Eighth Street
Stroudsburg, Pennsylvania 18360

ISBN 979-8-3313-1908-3

9 798331 319083

CURRAN ASSOCIATES INC.
proceedings.com